SMALL BUSINESS TOOLKIT

Marketing for the Self-Employed

MARTIN EDIC

© 1997 by Martin Edic

PRIMA PUBLISHING and colophon are trademarks of Prima Communications, Inc.

Library of Congress Cataloging-in-Publication Data

Edic, Martin.
    Small business toolkit : marketing for the self-employed/Martin Edic.
       p. cm.
    Includes index.
    ISBN 0-7615-0592-X
    1. Self-employed. 2. Marketing. I. Title.
  HD8036.E35   1996
  658.8—dc20   96-41172
                                        CIP

97 98 99 00 01 HH 10 9 8 7 6 5 4 3 2

Printed in the United States of America

How to Order

Single copies may be ordered from Prima Publishing, P.O. Box 1260BK, Rocklin, CA 95677; telephone (916) 632-4400. Quantity discounts are also available. On your letterhead, include information concerning the intended use of the books and the number of books you wish to purchase.

Visit us online at http://www.primapublishing.com

CONTENTS

ACKNOWLEDGMENTS

The knowledge in this book was gleaned both from educational sources like books and classes and from people, specifically self-employed small business owners. I learned my marketing skills from watching and doing, listening and taking action. Skills are the result of taking action. I'd like to thank all the self-employed people I've worked with over the past 20 years.

I'd also like to thank my editors at Prima Publishing for their incredible patience and general sense of enjoying their work; my wife, Annie Wells; and my business partners, Steve Forney and Casey Walpert.

Introduction

Making Contact
and Taking Action

The subject of marketing has an ominously big-business ring to it. The word itself conjures up images of blue-suited executives with voluminous strategic plans and arcane formulae for selling the latest widgets to an unsuspecting public. For the self-employed businessperson, marketing may seem much too complex. After all, what you really want is interesting, profitable, steady work doing what you do best. You don't need market research, strategic planning, and a slew of powerful tactics at your fingertips. Or do you?

Marketing for the Self-Employed puts these very effective marketing tools into the hands of the smallest business owners of all: the self-employed. Marketing is not complex when you reduce it to the basic process behind the hype. Marketing is communication designed to inform, convince, and sell. It includes everything from casual shoptalk to elaborate brochures and expensive advertising. For some, a few phone calls a week is all the marketing they need; for others, a more complete set of tools will be necessary to reach their best potential customers. In either case, you should know what you are selling, who has a need for it, and how to reach them. This book will help you learn these things.

To communicate and market effectively, you need to accomplish two things: You must make contact and you must take action. Sitting in your office or store and waiting for people to come to you won't work. You have to get out and tell people what you do and how they can benefit from it. Doing this requires a simple step: doing something to help your business. As simple as it seems, the principal marketing problem I've encountered in working with numerous small businesses is inaction. Call it *marketing paralysis.*

Marketing paralysis occurs when the business owner knows they need more business, knows that there are many ways to reach out and get it, but cannot make a move. Blocked by fear, insecurity, laziness, or a dozen other excuses, they do not act. And meanwhile, time goes by and the resources they started out with dwindle away; the business drive loses momentum. This brings me to the secret message that I hope pervades this book: All you have to do to be successful in your marketing is to *do something*. What is that something? Make contact with a potential customer.

Actions build on one another. My guess is that you became self-employed through a series of seemingly insignificant actions. A hobby gradually grows into a business. A skill becomes known and friends start to ask you to paint their house, give them financial advice, or help their business set up a computer system. You retire or get downsized out and your former employer calls one day and asks you to come back to work as a consultant. In some inexplicable way, you have jumped into the American dream of owning your business, through the effect of a series of actions.

Before I go any further, I'd like to give an example of the action and contact concept. If you've been in business for a while, have you ever called every one of your former customers and asked why they no longer do business with you? This action may prove a challenge, particularly as you get started, but you'll learn an immense amount and you will undoubtedly pick several of those customers up again. There's a simple reason why: It's a 99 percent likelihood that none of your competitors have ever called and asked for these customers' input the way you have.

If you're starting out, there is a similar action you might try. Call everyone you know, tell them you're going into business for yourself doing whatever-it-is and ask for their advice. This will accomplish several things. You'll start getting the word out. It will be easier than calling strangers and you'll get a little practice talking about your business, a valuable marketing skill. Most important, you'll be involving every one of these people in the future success of your business. They will want to see you succeed because you came to them early for help. The result will be referrals, references, and business.

A simple action like picking up the phone and calling people you already know is a powerful marketing tactic. Putting together a plan to coordinate this and a few other similar tactics can be all most self-employed people need to successfully market themselves. *Marketing for the Self-Employed* offers a process for assembling and implementing that plan, no matter what business you're in. All you have to do is take the first step!

SMALL BUSINESS TOOLKIT

Marketing for the Self-Employed

SECTION ONE

CREATING AN EFFECTIVE MARKETING PLAN

CHAPTER 1

THE MARKETING CHALLENGE

The day you decided to go out on your own and make a living by your wits, skills, and experience, a fundamental thing changed: No one else would guarantee you a paycheck every week, rain or shine. Only your efforts would determine whether you had money for bills, luxuries, business expenses, and the zillion other financial demands made on all of us in a society organized around money.

This change is the most frightening thing about self-employment—and the most liberating. The fear is understandable. The liberation comes from the knowledge that you can make your own choices and choose the direction of your own work life. You no longer have to stick to a nine-to-five schedule. When I made the decision to become a freelance writer and business consultant ten years ago, this freedom from a schedule was most appealing. A conversation with Pete McGrain, a friend who is a stained glass artist, clinched it. I ran into him one late spring morning in the parking lot of a loft building filled with artists' studios. He was loading two sailboards onto the roof of his car and I commented on how nice it was to be able to sail on a workday. He said that having the freedom to take a morning off was a major motivation for being self-employed. He was quick to add that taking that morning off meant pulling an all-nighter because he was up against a deadline for a piece he was working on. As he drove off to the beach, the appeal of being on my own was strong; I made the decision then and there to go for it.

Looking back, I know that his casual description of his life that day was more complex than it seemed. In a few sentences he mentioned scheduling, deadlines, his responsibility for a major work commitment, and the fact that there was a trade-off for his flexibility. If he played now, he'd make up for it later. Pete has made the self-employed lifestyle work, becoming an internationally recognized glass artist and still finding time for travel and sailboarding.

Ten years ago, I attributed his success to a free-wheeling state of mind and natural talent. Now I know that he is a superlative salesman and marketer in addition to a skilled glass artist. When he travels, he is often combining a trip with a lecture, a meeting with a client, or a master class to teach. His love of sailboarding has led him to move to the Columbia River gorge area of Oregon, a mecca for sailboarders. That windy mecca also happens to be a hotbed of glass artists, galleries, and collectors. Pete has integrated his marketing, his interests, and his art in a way that is a great example of the potential of being self-employed. His story also leads to the fundamental premise of this book.

When you choose to go on your own and become self-employed, you immediately face the challenge of finding customers or clients for your work. (Throughout this book I will be using the word *customers* rather than clients or buyers. It is a convenience. Feel free to substitute your own descriptive term.) Without a steady stream of customers, you'll have no money coming in. Without a constant marketing effort, you won't get those customers and you will be out of business. It is as simple as that. You cannot sell something no one knows or cares about. Marketing is the tool that you use to tell the world about your skills, experience, products, and problem-solving abilities.

Marketing is communication. It is also a necessary part of every action you take as a self-employed person. *Where* you do business affects your customers' decision to buy from you. *What* you sell determines who those customers are. *How* you respond to questions, complaints, referrals, and compliments determines whether customers continue to do business with you. *When* you respond often determines whether you get their business. *Who* you are and how you are known has much to do with your ability to earn.

Being self-employed is a choice—and it means taking responsibility for making more choices every day. No one will choose what you work on and when. No one will choose who you work with. You'll face these decisions every day. And every single one of those decisions has a marketing component. Pete could choose to go sailing because his experience told him that he was on schedule. It also told him that he could get the work done at night because he was single and his work was not dependent on the daily schedule of others. When he chose to move to the Pacific Northwest, his decision included the knowledge that he was moving into an area that is highly receptive to glass artisans. The decisions you make, no matter how different, also have a marketing angle.

YOUR MARKETING ATTITUDE

In this book, we'll look at many aspects of marketing—from planning to the nuts and bolts of writing an ad or producing a new product. There are an incredible number of options to choose from when it comes to marketing yourself. It can be confusing and overwhelming. To make the whole process easier, I'm going to tell you the one thing that I sincerely hope every reader takes away from this book. It's not a tip or technique, although there are many here. It's a simple change in the way you view your business. I call it your *marketing attitude.*

Your marketing attitude is a part of you that looks for the marketing opportunities and angles that are part of each decision you make as a business owner. It is something that develops with experience. It is the voice that tells you that this deal isn't right while that low-paying project might be worth taking. It's the voice that speaks in your brochures, letters, or seminars. It's the way you answer the phone, respond to requests for information, quotes, or assistance, and the way you cope with problems. It is the attitude that looks for ways to turn disaster into opportunity.

Developing this marketing attitude and integrating it into your working lifestyle is my goal as the writer of this book. My own experience as a self-employed person has not always been positive. I have learned from experience when to say no and when to take a chance. I have also learned that until you have a clear idea of what you want and how you're going to get it, you won't be happy as a business owner. The first part of *Marketing for the Self-Employed* is about finding out what you want and planning the marketing you need to achieve it. The standards and goals you set for yourself will determine everything you do and how well you succeed at it.

FREELANCE FOR HIRE

The word *freelance* comes from the Middle Ages, when wandering mercenaries would hire themselves and their weapons (lances) out to anyone who had the money to command their services. I imagine their lives were not as glamorous as they sound. Driven by hunger and the need for shelter, these medieval freelancers probably led an aimless existence, going from one master to the next. As modern freelancers, we face a very real potential for this kind of aimless existence. Many self-employed people work from job to job, paying the bills but unsure of where the next work will come from. They have limited earning ability because they can only do so much work per day and they can only charge rates that fit into the marketplace.

This kind of self-employment is often worse than the steady jobs they left behind. Instead of using all their skill and energy to perform the work they excel at, they waste much of that energy worrying about the near future and griping about the kind of work they were forced to take to survive. It is the dark downside of being self-employed.

Other self-employed people seem to have a very different experience. They enjoy their work and keep busy with interesting and lucrative projects. They have found ways to build momentum into their business that brings in a steady flow of new customers. They are always thinking about new products they can create that will leverage their abilities and raise the income ceiling imposed by a 24-hour day. They enjoy their work and thrive even when the occasional problem comes up.

The difference between the mercenaries and the visionaries has little to do with education or ability—and less to do with money. The visionaries have a plan. They have a set of goals they'd like to achieve and a concrete idea of how they are going to accomplish them. They see ahead to the next few years instead of the next few weeks. The mercenaries, on the other hand, have a clouded vision. All they know is that when things wind up with this little war, they'll head back into the dark woods to seek the next. They listen avidly for rumors of a neighboring kingdom that requires their services. Often they wind up without a roof in the dead of winter.

VISION AND CHANGE

Developing a vision is not a touchy-feely concept—it is a matter of survival. We live in a period of accelerated change that is unlikely to slow down during our lifetimes. In times of rapid change, the most valued skill is the ability to make informed decisions and act on them. This is precisely what the successful self-employed person excels at. The only way you can effectively make decisions is to know the facts and to view them in light of a bigger picture. That bigger picture is the personal goals that you have set for yourself.

Choosing goals and planning a route to attain them is a fluid process. You aim yourself in a specific direction and use that direction as a starting point. Along the way, things change and you adapt your goals to fit the new environment, sticking to the underlying ideas they represent. This is the first step in your marketing education. In the next chapter we're going to look at your personal marketing plan, the one that guides your business marketing plan.

CHAPTER 2

THE GOALS PATH: YOUR PERSONAL MARKETING PLAN

Two visions drive any successful business, large or small. The first is the vision of the owners of that business. Their goals, desires, dreams, and determination are the essential components of that vision. The other vision that is critical to the success of a venture is the vision of the customers. It too is composed of goals, desires, and determination. Discovering those goals is critical to successfully marketing your business.

These two driving visions combine to create a path that your business must follow to succeed. Your vision drives you internally to do good work, seek interesting ways to employ and improve your skills, and achieve the quality of life that you desire. Your customers' vision is what makes them buy your services or products—and it too is an internal, subconscious process. To reach into that process, you need an on-going set of plans that helps you discover your vision and how it interacts with that of your customers. In this chapter, we're going to look at your *personal marketing plan,* a process that helps you decide your direction and goals. In the rest of Section One, we'll look at your customers and build a marketing plan for your business.

THE GOALS PATH

Goals are targets. They are signposts. They are motivators. They help you refocus on the big picture when you're overwhelmed by the little one. They are not written in stone. They adapt. They change as you grow and change. They seldom have the same meaning when you achieve them as they do when you choose them. Their ultimate importance is to give your life direction and focus. By the time you reach them, you're already looking beyond to new goals. It is the path you follow to achieve your goals that is the gist of life, the flavor and experience. The walk is more important than the destination on the goals path.

An old Japanese proverb with parallels in many cultures says that the journey of a thousand miles starts with a single step. Because we live on a small planet, it can truly be said that every pathway is connected to the one outside your door. Step out onto it and you can make your way to any destination you choose. Choose a difficult destination and you will need many resources and much experience to get there. Choose a simple destination and the travel will be simple. Reaching your goals is much the same. No matter how unreachable a dream may seem, it is possible to find and follow a path to it. Ordinary people do it every day.

Many of us avoid choosing goals because we fear making the wrong choice. What we fail to understand is that inaction is a choice. If you don't choose your own goals, the world will choose them for you and you may not be happy with the results. Choices will be made one way or the other. Choosing your own goals increases the likelihood of success manyfold over the random approach. This brings us to the first guideline for choosing goals:

■ *They must be your own personal goals.* As alluring as the lives of others may be, your life must be driven by your own interests and desires. When someone else sets the standard, you'll never be fully invested in your own success. The fact that you have chosen to go out on your own as a self-employed person means that you have some understanding of the value of this rule.

When you define your goals, describe them in the first person. "I will have my product line in twelve stores by next Christmas." "My consulting practice will have an excellent reputation for turning around companies by 199-." If you have partners, each should write personal goals and then develop a set of goals for your partnership personalized with a "We" statement. "We will be the top graphic design agency in town two years from now."

The second guideline for choosing goals is:

■ *Use perfect world statements.* Perfect world statements start like this:

"If this were a perfect world, I. . . ."

Start out with fantasy. Give yourself goals far beyond your resources and knowledge. In a perfect world, I could charge $150 an hour for my work and deserve it. In a perfect world, I'd live in a house overlooking the ocean and create multimedia games that teach and inspire. In a perfect world, I'd be able to travel and earn a living anywhere on the planet. In a perfect world, I'd have wonderful customers who sent me interesting projects and appreciated the quality of my work.

These statements serve one major purpose. They take you out of the present with its familiar limitations, and they give your subconscious free rein to tell you about your dreams. At this point it is perfectly all right to fantasize. No one need see your fantasies, ever. These fantasies tell you something about your potential and the potential of your plan.

The third rule of goal setting is:

■ *Put it in writing.* Things look different when you put them on paper. They take on a presence of their own, and you are able to look at them a little more objectively. And writing is a physical act. In a very real sense, you take the first step toward realizing your goals when you write them down. They begin to take on momentum. At the end of this chapter, I'm going to give you a model you can use for setting goals. Using this model and pen and paper or your computer, you can take this first small step. At this point, you may want to keep a few notes about your perfect world goals in your planner, journal, or anywhere else that you can dedicate space to your personal marketing plan.

The next rule of goal setting takes you to the next level:

■ *Goals must be specific and detailed.* Remember how, as a child, you could pretend your way into any situation? You not only immersed yourself in your pretend world, you populated it with people, things, places, events, and actions. And, if you were like most kids, you were adamant about these details. This toy represented this, this corner of the room was this place, your imaginary friend's voice sounded like this. Once you've identified a few perfect world goals, start to fill in the details.

These details should include all the senses. Make your goals visual, auditory, tactile—or kinetic, full of smells, and even tastes. How warm is it? How bright is the lighting in your perfect workspace? Is it quiet or bustling with energy? These sensory details tell you a lot about what it would be like to live your goals on a real-world, day-to-day basis. They also tell you something about your future. If it's quiet and solitary, you will probably be working alone. If it's full of hustle and bustle, you may be working as part of a team at a busy worksite.

You also detail your goals by answering the who, what, where, when, why, and how questions. As you'll see when we start working on the marketing strategy for your business, these questions are vital to understanding why customers buy and what you will be selling, among many other considerations. In your personal marketing plan, they start to tell you what kinds of resources you will need to assemble, where you may need to go, and who you'll be working with. All these things tie into your entire life, so their importance as part of your goals is vital.

Once you've started to sketch out your goals, filling in detail and giving them dimensions of real life with a full set of sensory information, it's time to step back. Ask yourself what these goals mean on a basic level. For example, if you're a teenager dreaming of owning your first car, you may really be thinking about the freedom that a car can offer you. As a young couple living in a small apartment and looking for a home, you're seeking stability and control. As a self-employed business owner envisioning a prosperous practice full of interesting projects, you're setting a goal of stretching your abilities and being rewarded for them. The artist visualizing the studio of his or her dreams and the entrepreneur planning a multimillion-dollar business both have to consider what they are really getting themselves into.

Is that studio going to create a huge financial burden distracting the artist from his or her work? Will that big company mean risking your financial security if it doesn't work out?

RISK CONTROL

These underlying meanings and considerations are a part of the risk control aspect of setting goals. Remember early in this chapter when I mentioned that many people do not set goals for fear of making the wrong choice? Part of the reason for planning is to lower the risk of spending years of your life on something that doesn't turn out the way you wished. This risk control is a vital part of the planning process. Notice that I used the words *risk control* rather than risk evasion. There is a proven correlation between risk and success. You must take some risks to go beyond your daily routine.

Risks are actions that can have varying and potentially unpredictable results. Taking risks exposes you to opportunity. Risks also mean potential problems. Risk control means understanding what the potential problems and rewards of an action are and having a plan for coping with either situation. You limit your exposure to risk by knowing what you'll do in various situations.

Risk is not always what we envision. Too much success is risky. Many businesses fail because they failed to plan for success, and when it came they did not have the systems and resources in place to cope with it. This is a very real aspect of marketing. If you work alone and your marketing is too successful, there can be a backlash of ill will as you have to turn down work or miss deadlines. By planning for that situation, you can be prepared to control it by having others help you, keeping your prices high enough to filter out some of the work, or simply reducing the amount of marketing contacts you make and focusing on the most lucrative and interesting. This risk control gives you options and enhances your professional image.

This example of an overly successful marketing plan shows how personal goal setting and planning can work in your business life. If, as part of your goal setting, you envision yourself working at certain kinds of projects, you'll start filling out the details of those projects. How much time will you want to dedicate to work? Can others duplicate your abilities, or are you a unique commodity? If your skills and experience are unique, you will have to limit the number of projects you take on and find other ways to leverage your abilities. If you can train others to do what you do, then you could take on multiple projects. Do you want to? Do you want to manage people? Or would you prefer to work on your own? These questions are vital when it comes to planning your marketing.

Considering risk is an important part of goal setting. One of the most effective risk control strategies you can follow is looking at the big picture. When you consider a risky project in light of your three-year plan, you have a new perspective on the amount of risk involved. Perhaps the worst-case scenario would be all right if it meant working with people you'd like to develop long-term relationships with. Working together against adversity builds strong bonds. On the other hand, maybe a risky job you're offered will divert your energy and finances from your longer-term plan. Even if it is potentially profitable, it may cost you too much in the long run.

Another important risk control method is to identify your tolerance for risk, set parameters, and put them in writing. Then follow these personal rules religiously. In his books *Market Wizards* and *New Market Wizards* (Harper Business, 1989 and 1992), writer Jack Schwager interviews exceptionally successful stock and commodity traders to learn the processes they use to earn astronomical returns on their money. The universal rule they all follow is to limit exposure to risk and have a strategy for getting out of situations that go against you. They have learned that a bad trade that you let run can sap all your resources while a series of small successes can build them. Nearly every interviewee has a written set of rules for controlling risk that they follow to the letter. And every one has a war story of a big loss taken when they broke their own rules.

Your risk control strategy is driven by your personal marketing plan. Having a clear set of goals and developing personal rules based on experience and learning gives you a yardstick to compare the merits of a situation. Use your plan to make the right choices in your life.

TURNING DREAMS INTO REALITY

Setting perfect world goals, filling in detail, and considering your tolerance for risk are the start of the goals process. Bringing those goals into perspective by linking them to the actions you can take now is the beginning of realizing those goals. Your personal marketing plan defines your goals, refines that definition, and then gives you a path to follow to achieve those goals. To find the first step that puts you on your goals path, you have to try the simple exercise in time traveling you'll find in the next section. Here's a little background first, though.

Time travel does not require a time machine or an overactive imagination. All you need is memory, history, observation, and imagination. Historians make it possible for us to recreate the past, and futurists make it possible to consider the potential of the future. A little internal pretending and visualization can make it possible for you to do a little traveling into your own future. And once you're there, you can look back and see the path you followed to get there.

For the skeptical reader, I'll offer a simple justification for this exercise. Your subconscious stores and learns from every piece of sensory information you absorb, whether it's intellectual or real. We are as affected by a compelling film as we are by a conversation at a bus stop. And the mythology of our past has many truths that resonate even in these very different times. Thus time travel is a kind of training run for the subconscious. It sets out the challenges and problems involved in achieving a goal in a compelling way. The subconscious takes this information and starts working on it, finding solutions, developing resources, and generating the confidence necessary to accomplish the goals.

If you read stories of successful people, you'll find that they inevitably had a vision of where they wanted to go and doggedly stuck to it through adversity and the distractions of early success. In fact, Napoleon defined greatness as an almost obsessive ability to stay focused on a long-term objective. In his case, it was to become emperor of France and conqueror of Europe. In the case of Winston Churchill, he spent an entire lifetime in pursuit of the prime ministership of Great Britain, rising to lead the country against Hitler after 40 years in government, many of them as an outcast. These extreme examples of dedication to a goal are a testament to the power of visualizing the future. Why not try it yourself?

The following set of steps is a model for developing goals based on the experience and work of many people. I make no claims to be an originator of the process, but can testify to its effectiveness.

DEVELOPING A PERSONAL
MARKETING PLAN

You have a certain amount of control over your destiny, no matter what your present or past circumstance. This section describes one way of exercising that control to define a potential future and take action to realize it. The first action you take is to travel forward in time to a point two or three years from now. This is done by imagining your life as you'd like to live it in a perfect world. One way to accomplish this is to imagine your ideal workplace. Where is it? When you go to work in the morning, are you walking to work, commuting via water taxi, having a relaxing short drive through beautiful countryside, or walking across your loft to your home office? Remember—there are no rules or restrictions on what you can imagine, so give yourself free rein. As you imagine this workplace, you can fill in details. It may be a restaurant on a waterfront or a stable full of horses. In any of these examples it is easy to fill in the sights, sounds, smells, and other sensory data that make up a strong and compelling sense of place.

This imaginary workplace automatically tells you something about the kind of work you will be doing, the people you might be working with, and the place your business will be located. That loft may look out on a busy street several stories below. That water taxi may carry you across a great river basin surrounded by a gleaming skyline. Your walk out to the horse barn might tell you you're on the edge of a great prairie. Because it's all in your mind, it can be anywhere.

This is not the frivolous daydreaming it may seem. We tend to end up in places and situations that are familiar and accessible. Doing a little time travel helps your subconscious to feel a little more at home with your goals. You can expand outward from your workplace and fill in the practical details of your life, including how your family fits in, the kind of money you need to make to support that lifestyle, where on the planet you may be in this future, and other vital details of your goals.

You can do this exercise over a few days, refining your future by considering the realistic demands it might make on your time and energy. Once you develop a more detailed idea of your potential working life, take out a notebook and jot down the following:

Three years from now I will be working at. . . .

Just sketch in enough information to form a possible outline and add in as many details as you can. Don't worry if you draw a blank. This just means you don't have enough information right now to fill in that aspect. For instance, you may not know how much money you'll need or if it is even possible to make that amount of money doing your future work. You may not even know what the work you are doing is! The reason I suggest starting with the environment is that it is often easier to imagine what a workplace looks and feels like than to define exactly what a future job might entail.

So what are you doing? Do you own the horses or just train them? Is your loft an artist's space or a businessperson's? Do you sit down in front of a computer or a lathe? Do you have co-workers, or are you working on your own? Do you open up a store front every day or work deep into the night on last-minute assignments? There are no wrong answers, only those that appeal to you.

As you create this place and step into work there, look around you. Are you making things or selling them? Or both? Are you solving problems for clients, creating original designs, or helping others learn how to do these things? Who is buying your skill or products? Whose problems are you providing solutions for? Do you know all your customers, or do strangers come in and out of your life, making brief contact? Are you working with other people on a daily or weekly basis, or only on rare occasions? What kind of people have you surrounded yourself with?

This is an important question. Who do you spend your work time with? Are you comfortable with corporate executives, or would you rather spend time with artisans who get their hands dirty every day? There are no wrong answers here. Populate your work life with the kind of people you would like as co-workers, resources, customers, or fellow business owners. Try to avoid limiting your horizons here. Expand the contacts you have into areas you don't reach now. After all, this is three years from now and you know more; you have more experience and a wider range of skills and acquaintances. Maybe you are working regularly with someone you admire and respect. Write down a description of the kind of people you'd like to be working with and for.

This exercise will be very helpful when we start working on your business marketing plan in the next few chapters. Because a great deal of effective marketing comes from personal contacts, the people you surround yourself with are a very important part of your success as a self-employed person. Choosing to work with positive, creative, and motivated people will help you achieve these states of mind and raise the level of your work and income. Surrounding yourself with negative attitudes or people with a poor self-image will have the opposite effect. In our imaginary time travel exercise, I recommend imagining yourself surrounded by people you admire and respect rather than those you may be comfortable with or feel superior to.

Money is an important aspect of setting goals because it represents a measurable level of success in many parts of our society. It also gives you a level of confidence and freedom that can mean having the ability to choose your destiny. You do not have to acquire money to achieve your dreams—but it doesn't hurt. For the sake of this exercise, I hope you'll put aside any reservations you have about money and view it as a tool that can help you move ahead.

Setting specific monetary goals is critical to the success of your business. In Chapter 8 we'll look at the role of money in your marketing in greater detail. For now, it is important to give yourself specific monetary goals for your personal income and your business income. Look at your imaginary workplace and consider the expenses involved. Don't start cutting them now, just guesstimate what kind of costs you'd incur in that site. I suggest rounding it off to a monthly figure including rent, utilities, salaries, and marketing expenses. Add on your income you'd like to be paid for your work. Again, don't limit yourself. This is a pretend exercise and you're allowed to fantasize a bit. Once you've paid your bills and yourself, add on a profit figure. This goes beyond salaries and represents the increased value of your business, money for reinvestment or retirement, or a nest egg for adverse times. We'll look at profit in more detail in my chapter on money because I've found that many self-employed people fail to consider profit as separate from salary, an important concept in building any business.

Adding up the figures, determine an annual gross income from your future business. Now add on 50 percent. We'll use this figure as a target in your market planning. In the process, we may determine that it is unrealistic or too low but for now it gives you a concrete number to work with. Take that number and divide it by 1500 to get an hourly rate that your business should be charging for the services you provide or a net sales figure after cost of sales if you sell products. (The

1500 figure represents 50 working weeks at 30 hours per week.) It works like this:

Annual overhead	24,000	
Annual salary	40,000	
Profit	9,600	(15 percent)
Total	73,600	
Plus 50 percent cushion	36,800	
Total third-year income	110,400	

$110,400/1500 = $73.60 per hour

In this example, you'd need to bill an average of 75 dollars an hour, 30 hours a week. You'd be doing pretty well to accomplish this because we've built in considerable leeway for unexpected situations. However, this $75 target figure will be very useful when making decisions about how and where to market yourself.

Take a few minutes to do this exercise yourself with numbers that seem realistic, *in the context of your imaginary work situation.* This is important and you must put it in writing. You now have a physical description of your workplace, the type of work you may be doing, the people you work with and for, and the income you are making three years in the future.

The next step is to look at this imaginary scenario and try it on for size. Does it feel right? Are you excited by the potential it carries? Maybe when you see it written in black ink in the harsh light of day it loses its appeal. This can be an extremely valuable lesson and an excellent time management exercise. Many people dive into goals they have not considered from the big picture and make themselves miserable, wasting years of their life in the process. A few days of daydreaming and a few hours of jotting down your dreams while taking a trip into the future may have saved you several years of your life.

If this exercise generates a set of goals that don't work for you, start changing what doesn't work. You'll be able to see the reasons more clearly when your dreams are in writing and adapt or eliminate those aspects that are uncomfortable or unrealistic. Once you've created a compelling future destination, reduce it to several specific positive statements of action. For instance:

"I will be a successful architect with my own practice specializing in restorations of commercial buildings from the thirties and forties. My business will be located in a restored factory on the waterfront and will be an open, creative atmosphere filled with natural light. I'll employ several creative people guided by a unified vision and talent. My personal income will be $100,000 per year and I'll build my business by reinvesting a portion of my profits every year in new technology and talent. We'll be billing our time at $250 an hour, so my clients will probably be corporate planners dedicated to revitalizing their company's real estate assets while enhancing their company's reputation. I'll spend $40,000 per year to reach these specific clients and to develop new niche areas of expertise that are both profitable and creatively challenging."

Can you imagine what a new architecture student coming out of school could do with such a well-thought-out vision of how to integrate her life and skills? By setting higher goals, they might transcend the typical low-paying entry-level drafting work that many architecture graduates face after six years of school. Is this kind of vision realistic? People achieve it every day in all kinds of businesses.

Getting to the point where you can clearly define the goals you have for yourself and your business is a major achievement. Yet it is one that requires little or no money, a small amount of time and energy, and a large amount of imagination and positive thinking. It will automatically increase the likelihood of your success by setting you apart from your competition. The road becomes much clearer when you have a destination in mind and a road map to reach that destination. In the remainder of this book, we'll look at how marketing can help you create that road map and take the step that starts your journey of a thousand miles.

CHAPTER 3

YOUR BUSINESS
MARKETING PLAN

Setting personal goals and putting them in writing gives you a target to aim for and a standard to compare your progress against as you take steps to achieve those goals. In your work, setting goals and developing a plan to reach them is equally valuable; in fact, the two plans are interdependent. Setting business goals that do not fit in with your personal goals is a recipe for disaster, yet this happens all the time and frequently causes either the failure of your business or a major disruption in the rest of your life. For example, if your personal plan calls for a move to another area in the next few years and your business plan has you starting a restaurant here and now, you have a conflict. You should consider this kind of conflict now—before you build a future for yourself and step into it.

Once you've used the exercise in Chapter 2 to start identifying personal goals, you'll find that those goals take on a life of their own. Wheels turn, creativity starts bubbling, and you find yourself working on ways to realize those goals. As a self-employed person, you'll see much of that action in your working world—so plan accordingly.

If you've ever tried to borrow or raise money for a business, you know that the first step you must take is to write an effective business plan detailing your goals, needs, projected income, and all the other vital aspects of a successful business. No bank or serious investor will even discuss lending money or investing without such a plan. A significant part of any business plan is a marketing plan that tells the reader how you will build your business and sell your product or service. This marketing plan is the business equivalent of your personal plan.

Whether you write a business plan and include a marketing plan as a component or produce a separate marketing plan, you'll be considering the same questions:

- What are my strengths and weaknesses?
- What do I have to offer?
- Who can use my services, knowledge, or products?
- Will they or can they pay enough for them?
- How do I reach them and how do I convince them to do business with me?

- And how can I get them to become valued long-term customers who will send me more business and valued referrals?

Your marketing plan must include answers to all these questions. Finding these answers will tell you a great deal about your business and your customers now, before you spend a lot of time actually working on them. This is because of the incredible power of leverage that comes with effective planning.

Planning and Time

It has been estimated that for every minute you spend planning any action, you save 8 to 12 minutes when you take that action. Spending a minute to save 12 in the future is a kind of investment—one that gives you a handsome return indeed. This is because planning is an extremely high-leverage activity. A small amount of effort moves a lot of obstacles out of your path when you plan.

You may already have a successful business. Or you may be starting out or contemplating a new venture. In either case, your time is your most valuable asset. No one has more or less than you and no one knows for sure what their allotment of time on this planet may be. It is the great equalizer. Even a billionaire has only 24 hours in the day. For this reason, you'll often find that successful people are very interested in time, where it goes, what they get in return for spending it, and how valuable it is. As we work on your marketing for your business, your appreciation for the value of time will increase. Anything you can do to increase its value becomes a high-priority activity. Planning is such an activity.

How valuable is it? I've worked with a company that spent $50,000 a year on magazine advertising that they didn't need. When we looked at their marketing, we found that ten personal contacts a month between their senior partner and their top clients was worth far more business than the small amount generated by their ads. And that senior partner was already spending ten hours per month dealing with ad media designers and other production people. By simply reorienting his activity, based on what their marketing plan told us, they not only saved $50,000 per year in potential partnership profits (and this money required a lot more sales to justify itself—in this instance around $500,000!), they increased both their business and their customer satisfaction level.

This example is equally relevant to a much smaller business. A one-person business that randomly tries and discards various marketing techniques will not last long. An ad here, a mailing there, a brochure that doesn't get used, a meeting you aren't prepared for, or a customer who wastes your time can all do damage to your small business in many ways. A marketing plan gives you a blueprint for all your marketing actions.

WHAT IS A MARKETING PLAN?

Marketing plans range in complexity from hundreds of pages of research and demographics (information about people and their habits) to a simple one-page action list. The first time around, the planning process is one of information gathering and learning from that knowledge. After that you'll be tweaking and adapting your plan as circumstances change. It becomes an on-going plan of action for building your business and its sales.

Strategy and Tactics

The goal of any marketing plan is to develop a strategy for reaching and maintaining your sales goals, now and in the future. This strategy is the overall focus and model for your marketing. For instance, a picture framing business owner may assemble her customer list, analyze what people purchased and asked for most often, find out that interior designers were her most lucrative and regular customers, and decide that her primary marketing strategy would be to develop regular ongoing relationships with the designers in town. Knowing that her strategy would focus on the designer market, she would then choose a set of tactics that would target this group and help her build relationships with them. These tactics are the tools of marketing and range from the expensive (advertising, for instance) to the inexpensive (networking). Because our picture framer knows the value of time, she also realizes that an apparently cheap activity like networking can eat up a lot of valuable time. Her plan helps her define which tactics will produce the most business with the most effective use of her resources.

Your marketing plan will come together as you read this book. I'll be looking at all of the elements that make up an effective marketing plan for a small business. I'd suggest reading through and taking notes when something strikes a chord or seems relevant to your situation. When you finish, you can go back and create a marketing plan for your business using the following outline.

Elements of a Marketing Plan

Every marketing plan should address all of these items. You may leave out various tactics or phase them in as needed, but all of the elements of the plan are important. Sometimes something as basic as the way you use the phone or the look of your business card can have an unexpected effect on a customer. By working from a complete marketing plan, you'll start to think of every aspect of your business from a marketing perspective, ensuring that you don't miss out on opportunities or waste time on dead-end activities.

Your marketing plan should have three parts:

PART ONE—*A look at your products and your customers.* This section should:

- Evaluate the knowledge, capabilities, products, skills, and services you offer.
- Describe the people who need these products. Would they be willing and capable of paying for them and how much?
- Describe where you find these people, as well as their habits, preferences, jobs, incomes, and so on.
- Define additional products and services can you develop in the future to offer to these customers.
- Define related groups of prospective customers you can sell to, in addition to your core group.

PART TWO—*A strategy for reaching and convincing those customers to buy.* This section should:

- Define the problems you offer valuable solutions for.
- Tell how you will describe or convey the value of those solutions.
- Create a strategy you'll use to get your message to your target group of customers and convince them to buy.
- Choose specific tactics you'll use to implement your strategy.
- Plan ways to grow your business or expand your income to achieve your personal goals in the future.

PART THREE—*A calendar and a budget.* This section tells you what you'll be doing and how much you'll need to spend in both time and money, and ensures that you make the vital follow-up that creates loyal customers and strong business relationships. When writing it you'll:

- Create a calendar of ongoing marketing action, day by day and month by month.
- Define a budget for your marketing actions and put it in the calendar.
- Plan a referral-request program and put it in your calendar.
- Set aside a regular time each month to revise and evaluate your marketing plan, making changes where necessary.

If this outline seems overwhelming, let's put it in perspective by creating a simple plan for a one-person business we'll call Joe's Painting Company (at least for now).

Marketing Plan for
Joe's Painting Company
Prepared by Joe Thomas

Overview

This marketing plan is designed to help my company increase sales by 50 percent in the next year and increase profits on those sales by 20 percent. I'll accomplish these objectives by targeting a specific niche business and by focusing my marketing efforts on a group of customers who have a need for very high-quality painting services and have the money to pay more for a higher level of skill and neatness.

SERVICES AND PRODUCTS

Joe's Painting Company offers the following services:

- Expert interior painting, specializing in high-quality trim and finish work.
- Wall covering installation and paperhanging.
- Minor repairs and prep work as part of the painting work.

Our specialty is high-end decorator quality work using the best finishes. We do not do low-budget repaints on apartments or high-speed commercial work. We offer prompt estimates and guarantee our work will be completed on schedule, and we take pride in exceptional neatness.

CUSTOMERS

Our ideal customer is a high-income couple living in the prosperous southeast suburbs of our town. They usually live in a slightly older house and often use interior designers when remodeling. They read magazines like *Architectural Digest* and *Elle Decor,* watch *This Old House* on PBS, and usually have professional careers. Their concerns when hiring a painter are quality, neatness, speed, and cost, in about that order. They buy equal amounts of painting and paperhanging services

(continues)

and expect minor wall repairs and careful furniture moving as part of the job.

We can reach these customers through referrals from interior designers and contractors, by advertising in the local weekly town newspaper, and by personal referrals from previous customers, friends, and business associates.

Potential additional products and services we are considering offering include installation of custom window treatments and refinishing old woodwork. Another related market for our services may be the companies our clients work for.

Strategy and Tactics

Our marketing strategy is to stress our skill, neatness, and reliability and to use every job as a springboard for at least two referrals. We will use a regular weekly ad to convey this message and meet twice each month with interior design professionals to explain and sell our services. Our goals are to generate a steady stream of high-paying work that also results in referrals from satisfied customers. As a secondary goal, we will develop our window treatment installation business by contacting retailers and using our designer contacts.

Calendar of Marketing Actions

We will stick to our marketing calendar no matter how busy we become. We recognize that marketing is an activity that generates returns in the future.

Daily: Respond to calls from ads, send out estimates with no more than a 24-hour turn-around, call designers for appointments, call former customers (once every six months) to check on their work and ask for referrals.

Weekly: Make a sales call to interior design firms and retailers of window treatments. Run ongoing ad in *The Smalltown Shopper* ($40.00 weekly). Send greeting cards on customers' birthdays with business card attached (send to their office whenever possible).

Monthly: Analyze number of calls from ads, follow up on sales appointments, and send thank-you gifts to bird-dogs (people who refer business to us).

Annually: Create simple capabilities brochure for sales calls and to leave with satisfied customers to generate referrals. Check success rate of ads and revise accordingly.

Money and Budget
We anticipate expenses in these ranges:

Daily: Postage, supplies, and telephone—$7.50

Weekly: Business lunches, mailings, and ad—$60.

Monthly: Thank-you gifts (two per month at $10 each, Tape measures with our logo)—$20.

(continues)

Annual: Brochure production and printing—$500.

Total annual expenses: $5615.00—$467 per
month. This comes out to about 10 percent of annual sales as planned.

Keeping It Simple and Focused

Joe's plan is simple and focused. He knows his market
well and has tailored certain aspects of his plan to market needs, in particular an emphasis on reliability and
quality over price. He has a reasonable calendar of actions that he can accomplish without taking away from
the time needed to run his business. He has identified
a potential new profit center in the window treatment
installation business that fits well with his current skills.
The only thing I would recommend changing about
this plan is the name of the business—another phrase
could do a lot more to reflect the quality level and pro-
fessionalism that are Joe's selling points.

Your plan need not be any more complex. As
a self-employed businessperson, you have a limited
amount of time that you can personally devote to your
business. Creating an overly complex or ambitious
marketing plan can result in too much business and un-

happy customers. If you stay focused on your core strengths and customers, you can charge more while doing the work you really enjoy. Keep it simple.

Using Your Personal Marketing Plan as a Guide

The next few chapters will help you create an effective and focused marketing plan like Joe's. While you're considering and making the many decisions involved, you may run into points where you're unsure which route to take. Use your personal plan as a guide. Does this action or that choice fit in with the overall goals you've created? The answer to that question can help you make better decisions about your future as a successfully self-employed person.

CHAPTER 4

THE THINGS YOU DO: PRODUCTS, SERVICES, AND SOLUTIONS

One of the biggest challenges you face as a self-employed person is knowing your core strengths. A house painter may claim painting skills, a graphic designer may consider herself an artist and a financial planner might see himself as a source of knowledge for his clients. And they could all be right—and yet be wrong from a marketing perspective. The things we know and sell are seldom what they appear. That's because we don't see our work from the customer's viewpoint.

Let's look at these self-employed skills from another angle:

■ The painter is selling the end of a remodeling project and a new, cleaner, brighter environment.

- The graphic designer is providing compelling images to help the customers get their message across.
- The financial planner is helping his clients feel prosperous, comfortable, and secure about an unknown: The Future.

These are all emotional solutions to real problems. They are also the key to understanding what your products have to offer in the marketplace. No matter what you do, sell, or teach, your product is the same. In fact, it can be said that every reader of this book is in exactly the same business. What is that business? You provide exceptionally effective solutions to the problems facing your customers.

Problems and solutions are why all businesses exist. A common guideline for business success can be summed up in that old cliché: *Find a need and fill it.* Yet many people go into business based on their own needs rather than the needs of others—and it can be a fatal mistake. How many times have you seen a business that just didn't seem to make sense? A store that sells one item (vacuum cleaners, for instance). A service based on a short-lived trend. Energy poured into developing an invention or product that has only a very limited market. People start businesses like these every day—they get caught up in an idea, never stopping to consider the customers who might buy into that idea. They've created a solution to a problem that either doesn't exist or isn't common enough to justify a business solely dedicated to that idea.

This chapter is about products and product development. Every business has products to sell. Whether you offer consulting services, hot dogs from a pushcart, or a line of computer equipment, you have products. The consultant's product may be his or her expertise and experience. He or she solves a specific problem. The hot dog vendor also solves problems: hunger, lack of money for a fancy meal, not enough time to eat, desire for fresh air, and so on. The computer equipment seller has products, too, although they may not be what they seem on the surface. You go into a store to buy a cable for your laser printer. You can probably buy it cheaper from a mail order catalog—but you aren't sure what you need and you want to be able to return it if it's not right. That store must understand that they are selling advice, convenience, and time savings for their customers. Price is secondary.

We're going to look at your products from a marketing perspective. As you go through this chapter, I hope you'll understand that you may discover that you are in a very different business from the one you thought you were in. That different business is the one your customers see and hopefully need. You may find that your products are not providing the solutions that your customers require or that you are trying to sell to the wrong set of customers. That information will help you fine-tune your solutions to the problems they resolve. You might change focus, rearrange priorities, or redesign your product mix to match your market. The results will be more sales at more profitable rates and more satisfied customers.

DEFINING YOUR PRODUCTS: THINGS? SERVICES? SKILLS? KNOWLEDGE? TIME?

Start the process by listing, in a column on the left-hand side of a piece of paper, each of the products, services, or abilities you offer your prospective customers. Leave room on the right for a second column. Be complete, listing every possible feature of your business—including actual things you sell, knowledge you've acquired, skills you've learned, past experiences, resources you can offer, any special equipment you have, your location, your previous accomplishments, and so on. Write down anything that seems relevant.

Like most of the exercises in this book, you'll find that I ask you to start with a wide range of things before you begin to make choices. This is important—if you filter up front, you may leave something out that is important in ways you don't understand right now. So don't be selective in listing your abilities. Empty the wastebasket on the floor and catalog everything in it.

It may help to do this with a friend or spouse who knows something about your business. With two people, you can do a little brainstorming, throwing out ideas and helping each other avoid any mental screening. Just get it all down on paper.

Now look at your list. I hope it's a long one with some silly or irreverent items included. Title this first list *Features*. Starting at the top, make a second column titled *Benefits*. Next to each feature, write down the corresponding benefit to your customer. A benefit is an actual valued solution to a real problem faced by your customers. That solution may be monetary, psychological, physical, or emotional. It may affect their livelihood or simply enhance their day. In contrast to the first list, you must be ruthless when determining benefits. If a feature item has no real value to your customers, draw a line through it. You may have a beautiful office—but if the client never visits that office, it's no longer relevant from a marketing perspective. (It may be very relevant from your perspective, but that doesn't matter here.)

Determining the actual or perceived benefits of your products and services gives you a valuable set of guides for your market planning. You may discover that you have been trying to sell features instead of benefits. I've seen many new business ads and brochures that list feature after feature without addressing the actual problems or desires of their market. I recently received a mailing from a new recording studio in my area. In their three-page letter, they spent 90 percent of the message telling me about every piece of esoteric audio equipment they own. Nowhere did they tell me how this gear would enhance my recording or make my music better. Because I own a studio myself and have spent a great deal of time in other studios as a client, I know that few musicians really care about equipment. They want to be comfortable and secure in the knowledge that the studio will capture the essence of their music. They want reassurance that they are working with skilled, insightful people. I've found that appealing to these concerns is a much more effective marketing strategy than trying to appeal to the same customers as though they were equipment buffs.

In all your marketing, from personal sales to advertising, you should never mention a feature of what you do without immediately describing its benefit to the customer. If you have a downtown office, always add that there's plenty of parking nearby or that you are right next to another business you know the customer is likely to frequent. On the negative side, if that downtown location works against you, you must offer a solution that alleviates the problem: Tell them you offer a pick-up and delivery service, extra hours, you'll come to them at their convenience, and so on.

If there are items on your worksheet that don't convey an immediate benefit or that you cannot easily overcome by offering another choice, eliminate them from your marketing. They don't interest your customers and may have a negative effect, driving customers away. This can work in ways that you may not expect.

For example, a local cabinetmaker decides to step up his marketing to attract better work. He has a beautiful brochure produced with professional photographs of his work, compelling copy, and an award-winning print job. It's a really nice piece of work. However, after he's been mailing and handing out the brochure for several months, word gets back to him that it's a disaster. It turns out that his best market consists of people looking for quality work at reasonable rates and that glossy brochure is scaring them away. It makes him look too expensive and exclusive. He has emphasized the wrong solutions for *his* customers.

Once you've identified the features of your business and the corresponding benefits to your customers, you can start to focus on your strongest products. Choose those items on the list that have the most compelling benefits. Look for ways that you can improve these products until they represent the best solutions available for that particular problem. This fine-tuning process is a vital, ongoing part of being self-employed. Every day you should be thinking about ways to make your products and services more compelling.

While you are evaluating what you do, you must consider your priorities. Some items on your list are more valuable than others. They represent a more lucrative market, a more interesting career, or an opportunity for personal growth. Ideally, you'll have things on your list that embody all of these things. I highly recommend that you focus most of your energy

on these highly effective products and drop some of
your less-appealing items.

YOU ARE A SPECIALIST

As a self-employed individual, you have a very limited
amount of time and energy. You are probably at your
best specializing in one or two areas rather than trying
to be all things to all customers. Fortunately, specialization has its rewards. It frequently pays more as you offer
experience and skills not generally available. It is much
easier to market a specialty because you can easily
target a small group of highly motivated buyers who
understand the value of your knowledge and products.
This targeted marketing can be much less expensive
than trying to draw in the whole community.

Specializing is the wave of the future in small
business. We live on a planet with a huge population
whose interests are wide-ranging. In the United States,
with a population of over 240 million, even the most
obscure interest group may support a number of small
businesses. There are trade magazines, conferences and
shows, Internet groups, and associations for a mind-
icant to an outsider. As a specialist you become an
insider, with inside knowledge and abilities that others
will want.

Running a small business, the self-employed person
probably doesn't need to reach that many customers.
You may only need to reach a handful of people to

keep yourself busy around the clock. Because of this small scale, many classic big-company marketing tactics don't make sense. Instead of mailing thousands of pieces of direct mail, you can focus on developing relationships that generate referrals. Because your products don't have to appeal to the multitudes, you can build in features that appeal to a specific market and charge more as a result.

What if you have a product or service that really has a wide market appeal? You probably do not have the resources to market it successfully yourself. This takes us right back to the specialists. Find the people who can market your product or knowledge and license it to them. Books that pay royalties, inventions that pay licensing fees, software sales, and public speaking engagements are all examples of ways to market your abilities to a broader audience. To achieve these things, you are still marketing your products to a small market. A writer markets to a small group of editors at publishing houses that can profit from the work. A kitchen gadget designer licenses her designs to a houseware manufacturer or a mail order seller. A consultant designs seminars, hires a speakers' bureau, and travels, giving presentations and selling his knowledge to a wider audience.

When you look at your product mix, you should consider the wider market potential of what you do. It may be possible to hand over the production and marketing to a bigger company with bigger resources in exchange for a royalty or fee. This is a marketing decision that you need to consider in light of your personal goals. It may be that the limelight is not for you. It may also be that you find that you love getting out and meeting or dealing with large numbers of people.

THE PACKAGE

We all know the power of a compelling package. A shiny box covered with eye-catching graphics can make a big difference in how your products move in the marketplace. This is true even if you only sell a service or your expertise. Packaging comes in many forms. It includes:

■ *Your personal appearance.* You should reflect the lifestyle and business style of your customers. One good rule is to dress up one level from the accepted norm for your business when meeting new clients. Once you've formed a business relationship, you can work on their level. This can work in odd ways. The CEO of a rapidly growing company once told me that he hoped he would never see me in a dark business suit because they saw me as a creative resource and expected me to dress more casually.

Part of packaging yourself is that all-important first impression. You are asking your customers to invest time, money, and energy in your enterprise. A professional appearance says that you're trustworthy. A sloppy or inappropriate appearance says volumes about your own work habits.

■ *The appearance of your business or work environment.* If you see customers at a place of business other than their own, it must be neat, attractive, and interesting. If you come to them, make sure your car is neat. Sweep the proverbial sidewalk in front of your store every day.

■ *Your marketing materials.* Logos, stationery, brochures, presentations, Web sites, and other visual marketing materials require attractive packaging to appeal to your target market. Studies show that more than 50 percent of us communicate visually, representing information as visual images in our minds. When you use poorly designed materials, you may be losing half your potential customers.

■ *Your telephone manner.* For one-person businesses, this can be a very important part of your packaging. Often you will be doing a major part of your marketing and selling on the phone. Answer it consistently and clearly with a calm, down-to-earth tone. Smile when you speak. People can tell. Always get the information and repeat it to avoid errors.

■ *Your business name.* Names are a vital part of the package. They can help a customer remember you or they can scare someone away. They can project an attitude, either good or bad. Great names are unique, easy to remember and pronounce, lend themselves to a corresponding visual logo, and tell something positive about your work. If you sell your personal knowledge and skills, use your own name unless it is difficult to remember or pronounce. Avoid clever names—they seldom age well. You want a name that you can build until it is the first one that your customers think of when they need your specialty. We'll be looking at identity components like names, logos, and taglines in detail in Chapter 9.

As you can see, packaging your products involves much more than a colorful bag or a nice business card. Big businesses spend zillions on the whole package because they know that they are building an asset that has long-term profit potential and increases the overall value of their company. The value of a name like Kodak or Coca-Cola is incalculable, and those companies spend millions every year keeping these vital assets fresh in the minds of their consumers. Even a tiny one-person business needs to develop long-term relationships with its customers. Putting together a compelling package for your skills and products is a vital first step.

THE PITCH: THE ONE-SENTENCE DESCRIPTION

Knowing what you do and why your customers need your business is fundamental to every aspect of your marketing. Thinking about your products and refining every aspect of them until they are at their best creates a strong foundation to work from when you go out into the world and start to market and sell. You know what you do and why. All you have to do is reach the right people and show them how you can resolve their problems. One final tool you can develop, for a small investment of your time, is your pitch.

The pitch is a sales tool and fits in with the whole selling process. We'll be looking at that process in more detail in Chapter 17. For now, you need to answer one question. Can you describe your business in one sentence? This one-sentence description will show up in all of your marketing actions from casual networking to expensive advertising (if your business calls for it). Coming up with a simple, brief description of your business is a challenge. You should describe what problems you can solve for who. For instance:

- *A business writer:* I'm a professional communicator who can clearly explain complex concepts.
- *A recording studio:* We help creative artists get great recordings of their music.
- *A sales rep:* We offer a complete resource for commercial welding and metal fabrication services.
- *A gift shop:* We help you find last-minute gifts for any occasion.

Sometimes the right name can achieve the same effect. One of my favorite names is a gift shop in my town called "The Eleventh Hour." The owner knows that her market is those last-minute gift buyers who no longer care about price as long as they can get a nice gift, wrapped and ready to go, right now. The name positions her shop as exactly the place you need in that situation. She solves the problem (procrastination or lack of time) while charging top dollar for the solution and keeping her customers happy.

Come up with a one-sentence description of your business that stresses the benefit and the solutions you offer, and you'll always have a ready answer when asked what you do. That simple sentence can be a very powerful marketing tool when used consistently.

Once you've come up with a one-sentence description of your business, practice it until it rolls out easily at the drop of a hat. Refine it until it is simple and memorable enough to be repeated by others. And use it. At social gatherings, networking events, when meeting new prospective customers, and any other time someone asks, "What do you do?" You'll find it showing up in your advertising and publicity, often as a brief tagline reinforcing your name. Eventually it will help establish you as the recognized source for whatever solutions you provide.

PROFIT CENTERS

While you're considering your products and ways to promote and improve them, you should consider your product mix. Once you've established a reputation and a market for one product, you may want to consider what related products or services you can offer to those same customers. By piggybacking additional products onto your core product you can increase sales per customer, easily improving your income while building an even stronger relationship.

You should be careful not to add unrelated products, however. Nothing will turn a customer off quicker than someone who tries to sell them some other unrelated service or item. If you install computers, offer to configure software, sell peripherals, train users, or similar related services. Don't try to pitch a new vitamin product or your cousin's restaurant. If you do, you'll see your hard-won credibility fade in their eyes.

Besides add-on products, there is another category of product extensions I call *profit centers*. Profit centers are related products or services that do not require substantial extra work or time. A public speaker or seminar leader sells books and tapes at a table at the back of the room. An interior designer handles a catalog line of ready-made window coverings. An accountant offers investment seminars. All of these profit centers work on several levels: They add to the bottom line by increasing cash flow and profits. They enhance the seller's reputation as an expert, leading to more primary business. And they leverage your time so that you can sell your expertise over and over again.

The concept of leverage and products is very important for self-employed people. Even if you are an expert consultant making $75 an hour, 30 hours a week, you know that your upside income depends on the number of hours you can actually bill each week.

You hit a ceiling at around $110,000 per year (not that there's anything wrong with that). But what if you assemble a workbook of your knowledge and sell it to clients you can't reach or who don't have the time or money for your personal attention? You sell the workbook for $100 and offer it at seminars or via mail order. You can hire fulfillment companies to handle the orders and even hire someone to put it together for you.

That $100 book may only appeal to a few thousand readers over the next few years—but it has the potential of doubling your income with much less work on your part. That's the power of leverage and profit centers. Other profit centers include reselling parts or related items with a markup, hiring work out to others and marking it up, or receiving referral fees from others.

The concept of leverage is vital to your success as a self-employed person because your most valuable resource, time, is also your most limited resource. Finding ways to sell your knowledge over and over again without having to be there in person is the secret to higher earnings. Products are a package of knowledge, experience, and skills that you can duplicate over and over again for sale to many customers.

You know those little caps on shampoo bottles that pop up to dispense the shampoo without a mess? There are dozens of variations on the basic idea and a lot of them come from one man working out of a home shop in New England. He specializes in packaging solutions for manufacturers of physical care products.

He invents a cap or bottle in response to an industry need, licenses the design for an up-front fee or royalties, and collects checks. It is said that he has standing orders to his accountant to let him know when he has made $250,000 in any year. At that point he stops working and pursues other interests. And he typically reaches that point in less than six months.

This story is a good example of following a personal goals plan (limiting his income and freeing up his time), developing a product that can be duplicated and sold many times, and focusing on a specialized market. He does all three very well and reaps a handsome reward for his efforts. That's the power of leverage, packaging, and knowing your products and markets.

CHAPTER 5

THE PERSONAL
CONNECTION:
YOUR CUSTOMERS

The finest product in the world is worthless when there is no market for it. Yet people invest enormous amounts of energy starting businesses for which the market is too limited to be, profitable. It is said that 90 percent of all new businesses fail. While I'm not completely convinced of that figure's truth, I do believe that the reason for the high failure rate is simple: People jump into a business without learning enough about their potential customers. They think about locations, products, concepts, money, and a host of other details. Unfortunately, every one of these business decisions and challenges depends entirely on your customers' needs and desires. Your success has nothing to do with your personal wants except as they relate to the way you serve your market.

Who will buy the problem-solving products you offer? The answers to that question are the keys to a successful marketing plan. Who are your customers, where are they, why would they want your help, and can they pay for it? You must have the answers to these questions before you spend any additional time or money promoting your business. In fact, it is vital to know these answers before you even consider starting a business. And if you're already in business and experiencing slow growth or a slump, you can often jump-start things by going back to the basics: Rediscover your customers.

The number one rule of small business marketing, in my humble opinion, is that you are always selling to individual people rather than to companies, demographic groups, neighborhoods, or any other groups of people. Even when your checks come from a Fortune 500 company, individuals authorize and sign them. Those people are the ones you must focus your marketing and customer service efforts on.

Identifying the individuals who can make your business succeed is the goal of this chapter. You need to understand how your business looks from their point of view. You need to know as much about their needs, desires, and problems as possible. You need to know where they are and the best means to reach them, one on one. And you need to orient your marketing plans to accomplish these things.

One of the most important marketing lessons successfully self-employed people learn is how small their real market is. You can be wildly profitable while dealing with as few as three different customers. Even one major customer can generate more than enough work for most self-employed people. The danger in relying on one customer is the "all your eggs in one basket" syndrome: That solitary customer can put you out of business with the stroke of a pen or a change in personnel.

If you only need to reach three people, then marketing should be a breeze, right? The challenge is to identify those key people, reach them, and convince them that you have solutions they need. And that can be a big challenge.

Right now, I can hear some readers thinking that they need a lot more than three customers to succeed. Well, maybe—that depends on what you're selling and how much repeat business you can hope for. But three will do when it comes to cold marketing. Consider master car salesman Joe Girard, who sold over 300 cars a year in the Detroit area working out of a 3 × 5 card file. Joe says that for every customer that you please you'll get 2 or 3 positive referrals—and for every customer you make angry you'll get 10 negative referrals. He goes even further and defines how wide a single customer's sphere of influence is by using the typical wedding invitation list as an example. The number of people a bride and groom would invite to their wedding is representative of how many people they influence with their buying experiences. If the average is 100 guests at a wedding, their range of close acquaintances is around 100. Using this unscientific but reasonably realistic example, it turns out that 3 loyal customers may influence up to 300 other potential customers.

I like to think of this in terms of a new store opening in your neighborhood. The first day three people who don't know each other walk in and buy something. They have a good buying experience and tell their friends about the store. This happens every day for a week. At the end of the week, using Joe's theory, that store has reached a potential market of 2,100 customers, all based on three successful sales per day.

Although overly simplistic, this story makes my point. By focusing on the best customers for your business and providing superlative service and products, then staying in touch and asking for referrals, you can build a strong business from very few contacts. In marketing, this is known as *targeting*—and it is the only proven marketing strategy there is.

TARGET THE KEY PEOPLE

Targeting takes the mystery out of marketing. Instead of being overwhelmed by the vast world of potential customers out there, you make an informed decision to go after a small but highly motivated group of *key people* who will buy, make referrals, and ideally become loyal supporters of your business. Targeting is the process of identifying these key people through research, learning about their needs through sales skills, and aiming your marketing directly at them and at the heart of their needs and desires.

We all like to meet people who have the ability to get to the core issue in any project or discussion. They save time and help us work at a higher level. Part of your targeting strategy involves discovering the key issues that your customers face and aiming your solutions (products) at those issues. You tailor what you do to the specific requirements of the buyer. To accomplish that, you have to have a clear understanding of that buyer.

Everyone knows about market research as a concept. As a reality, it often seems beyond the means of the average self-employed person. After all, you don't have a large staff, access to expensive resources like consultants, databases, and focus groups, or a budget to afford these things. Or do you?

Ninety-five percent of the customized market research tools and resources available to large companies are available to you for free. Those big companies pay for the research and get the first fruits of their investment, often tailoring their research in very specific ways. Very shortly afterward that research comes out in places like magazines, published studies, newsletters for special interest groups, Internet sites, books, and seminars open to the public. We live in an information economy, and that means that more information is available for less effort than ever before.

So where do you start? Once again, you start with the basic questions—who, where, why, what, and how. If you've opened a housewares store specializing in high-end kitchen equipment for serious cooks, you obviously have an idea of what your market is. How do you reach it? You start by going further and considering the lifestyle of your individual customers. Who are they? You might start by considering what they read. If they subscribe to gourmet cooking magazines, you can call a magazine's advertising sales rep and ask for an advertiser's media kit using your company name. They'll send you a package of sales materials and ad rates for their magazine. Somewhere in that folder, you'll find comprehensive demographic profiles of their reader base. These demographics are a specific description of your customers—their incomes, education, interests, and so on.

This technique can work for many businesses, once you've identified a common publication or association your customers might be involved with. Associations and industry groups are valuable sources of research. They often have public relations departments dedicated to spreading the word about their activities, members, and issues. You can find out about the mind-boggling number of special interest associations out there by heading to the library and asking for the *Encyclopedia of Associations.* Look up your subject and make some calls requesting information on their group.

Your public library is an obvious place to do research. I've found that many of my small business clients never set foot in their local library in spite of the fact that a few minutes of research can save them literally thousands in lost business, consulting fees, advertising expenses, and a host of other marketing-related costs. A regular trip to the library is one the highest-leverage marketing actions you can take—whether you're a house painter or a computer programmer.

The challenge for library-phobes is knowing what to ask for. If you're unsure, just walk up to the information desk, tell them you're Joe Painter or Samantha CodeWriter and that you're trying to find out more about the customers you do business with. It's as simple as that. Librarians don't get their degrees in library science anymore, they get them in information management—and they love to help people find the right info. They know about databases, indexes, how-to books, and zillions of other resources that can tell you more than you ever wanted to know about your customers.

In fact, it can be overwhelming. That's why you need to zero in on a few specific questions you need answers for. I'll give you one to start with: "Where can I find five names of people who are likely to have a strong need for my services or to know people who do?"

Getting the answer to that question is a great marketing exercise. In fact, it may be the only marketing action you need to get started or to build up an existing business. That's because the process of answering that question and using that answer can mean a lot of business. And if it's not enough business, you can always go back for more names.

FIVE NAMES THIS WEEK

Putting together the names and profiles of five potential customers may not seem too easy at first. That's fine. Start with any names of people you already know who haven't bought anything from you. Look at those names and ask yourself if they are really good prospects for your business. If you can't answer that question, consider going right to the source: Give them a call, tell them you're working on marketing your business and ask them if you can pick their brains. Don't try to sell them anything! Information and perspective are what you seek. The selling comes later.

Tell them briefly about your business. Then ask the following questions, adapted to your service or product. Listen and take notes. Don't interrupt or express opinions. Act like those dispassionate people who call you with surveys—just listen and record.

- Do you currently buy [hire, contract for, outsource, shop at, whatever] a service like mine?
- What do you look for when making a buying decision?
- What is the most important benefit to you of [service, product, whatever]?

- What would you like to see improved about [service, product, whatever]?
- What related products would you like to be able to get from the same source?
- How much, approximately, do you spend per year on [service, product, whatever]?
- Where do you hear about your resources, suppliers, contractors, whatever?
- How often do you make referrals and what do you consider before referring someone?

Keep the conversation short unless the person wants to talk. Consider only asking one or two questions per call or visit. Follow up with a thank-you letter and a small gift as a consideration for picking their brains. A book, tape, or other information source is a good choice. Don't scrimp; get something of real value. Whatever you do, don't sell! This is not the time. And listen, listen, listen. Listening, rather than talking, is the number one sales skill. Your customers will voluntarily tell you things you'd never get from probing if you let them go at their own pace. Take an interest in their advice and make sure you let them know how much you value it.

The primary goal of this exercise is to gather information. You will make sales and get referrals as an extra bonus, if you listen and follow up. Once you have the info from several calls, look at your notes and look for trends—common areas of interest and concern—

and list them. These issues will define much of your marketing message.

An informal research project like this can yield a great deal of valuable business, especially if you take it to the next step. As you develop contacts with a number of people whom you've questioned about your business, enlist those who take the most active interest and keep in touch with them. Its likely that they are getting as much benefit from your relationship as you are.

Besides acting as a research method, this practice of enlisting supporters and information resources is a powerful marketing tool. If you make five of these calls per week or even five per month, you'll soon find that you've created a network of key people who have made a small personal investment of time in your business. You'll share resources, contacts, and experience—and the result will be sales and referrals. If you keep your ears and mind open, you'll gain serious insight into why your business is prospering or not.

EXPANDING THE KEY PEOPLE LIST

Once you've started the process of learning about your business from your customers, you can go to the next step and formalize your list of key people. Ask if you can maintain contact with them periodically to pick their brains. Offer to make referrals to them whenever possible. Put together a mailing list of your key people and make sure they learn first about new developments in your work. Add people to the list from your suppliers, professionals you work with like lawyers, accountants, realtors, and salespeople, as well as friends, family, and other interested persons.

Developing a core group of key people who act as informal business advisors is a vital marketing tool to small business owners. Not only are they a source of knowledge and experience, but they offer the best source of business for any self-employed person: *referrals*. We'll be covering the subject of referrals in detail in Chapter 18.

It would be easy to go much further with the subject of defining your customers. Demographics, customer profiling, targeting, and other research techniques show up in exhaustive detail in many publications devoted to the subject. In Chapter 12 we look at direct response marketing and developing a customer list in more detail.

Ultimately, you must come to understand what motivates your customers. Any advertising copywriter will tell you that the best ad writing comes when you can imagine yourself carrying on a direct and personal conversation with the reader of the ad. Making personal contact is the key to any successful small business marketing plan because it personalizes you and your business in the minds of your customers. They're no longer dealing with a supplier; they're dealing with Jane or John who knows their needs and always comes through for them. That personal connection is what builds long-term relationships and future business.

Your customers and your prospective customers are looking for people they can trust and rely on when they choose to do business. Because you are your business, this gets very personal. With self-employed people, the borders between work and home will be blurred because very often it is you that is being hired, not your business or skill. For this reason, a primary goal when marketing any self-employed business is to make it as personal and one-on-one as possible. This doesn't mean being buddies with all your customers; it means establishing a relationship that is mutually beneficial.

The concept of mutual benefit is vital to the success of any business—but especially so for a one-person business. If you rip off your customers, you'll only get their business once and they'll tell everyone to avoid you. You'll be reinventing the wheel every day as you seek new rubes to pull your scams on. When you add value to your customers' lives and make them feel that you have each gained from the transaction, you'll both feel good about making referrals to each other.

THE EMOTIONAL CONNECTION

Personal connections are emotional connections. You and your customers share an interest. Making an emotional connection is an important part of your marketing message. Remember the recording studio that tried to use equipment as a marketing pitch? That message had no emotional resonance with its intended audience. Musicians are creative people and they tend to find recording an intense and sometimes frightening process. By positively addressing these emotional issues (achieving creative potential and reducing fear), the studio would have made an important emotional connection with its potential clients. They would feel that they could relate to the people who wrote that material much better than to the technician who wrote the letter in the example.

Words like emotion, feeling, and connection do not pop up frequently in standard business texts, but they are a mainstay of effective marketing. For the self-employed, that emotional bond means referrals, long-term business relationships, new resources, and an ongoing learning experience that enhances your life—all excellent reasons for making that connection. Above all, remember that customers are always individual people just like yourself, not massive demographic groups in some remote computer database.

CHAPTER 6

STRATEGY AND THE EMOTIONAL MARKETING PLAN

Understanding what you sell and who will buy it is the foundation of any marketing plan. The structure you build on that foundation is determined by an overall blueprint for going out and generating business. That blueprint is your strategy. Once you've decided on a strategy, you'll choose from the various tactics available to put your marketing plan into action.

Any strategic plan has several components. You'll target an audience. You'll tailor your product to that audience. You'll tell them about it. You'll involve them emotionally. And you'll close the sale. And then you'll follow up to generate additional sales and referrals and keep your valued customers happy. This is not a cold analytical process, no matter what the MBAs with their marketing formulas tell us. To the contrary, it is an emotionally charged process filled with fear, exhilaration, disappointment, and other rides on the emotional roller coaster.

If emotions and business seem strange bedfellows to you, you're not alone. *Businesslike* has always meant logical and analytical. This is one of the biggest myths of the American Dream and it is embodied in the image of the hard-boiled, cigar-chomping person who is "strictly business." Scratch this myth and something unexpected happens: Under that hard-boiled exterior is a human being doing a job and experiencing all the fears and stresses that come with it. Reach those emotional humans, offer a solution that dissolves those fears and that stress, and they will buy. And you'll be their savior and champion.

Developing an overall strategy starts with an understanding of the psychology of what you do for others. It's not mumbo-jumbo or New Age rambling; it's a concrete description of the emotional and logical reaction to your marketing. If your customers buy out of fear of failure, you must sell them guaranteed success. If they buy on an excited impulse, you must keep them excited about your product long after the sale. If they are nervous and indecisive, you must be calming and help them make informed decisions they can live with. Ignore the underlying emotional content and you'll fail to sell just when you think you've made it.

Fear

It is tempting to focus on fear as a marketing strategy because basic fears are often very effective human motivators. Fear of loss, fear of appearing inept or foolish, fear of being alone and unsupported, fear of failure, and the many other fearful emotions and situations all make tempting sales targets. Yet there is a catch. When you buy based on fear, you're only temporally evading your problem and you'll ultimately feel bad about your purchase as the temporary feeling of respite dissolves. Use fear to sell and you will not develop the repeat business that is necessary to the success of most self-employed businesses.

Positive Versus Negative

There is a simple reason for avoiding fear as a marketing strategy. It has to do with the fundamental way our brains process information. We tend, on a subconscious level, to process instructions quite literally as we receive them. Because of this logical reasoning we have to imagine an event before we can negate it. If I say, "Don't think of the color blue," you must create a mental image of the color blue before you can put it away. It's simply the order in which we think.

When you play on a person's fear in order to sell him or her a solution for that feared event, you are reinforcing that fear and associating it with you and your product. They must experience the fear you lay out for them before they can experience the relief of having a solution at hand. And in the long run, they'll subconsciously avoid you and your business in order to avoid reliving their fears. You must use positive images and language in all of your marketing.

We've all heard of the power of positive thinking, and those steeped in skepticism might say that the world is a tough place that you can't ignore by pretending to be upbeat and positive. In fact, we have no choice. Positive thinking is a quicker way to process information than negative thinking. Every irony, negative statement, negative image, or discouraging thought you embed in your marketing is a roadblock to the final decision to buy or do business with you. The positive path is the clear path.

PROBLEMS AND SOLUTIONS

Fortunately, the positive is also the easiest to formulate for your business. Your product or service solves a problem or problems for your potential customers. They are aware of the problems on some level. For this reason, the most effective marketing strategies identify the fundamental problems your customers face, demonstrate the solutions you offer, tell the customers about those solutions, and then make it easy to purchase those solutions. These messages help the customers make the decision.

Let's look at these criteria as guidelines for creating your marketing strategy:

1. Define the problem or problems your product [service, whatever] solves.
2. Define what groups of people have a pressing need for your solutions and the ability to pay for them.
3. Decide how to reach those customers effectively.
4. Reach out and tell them about the solutions you offer, before you detail the problems. This is a seeding stage that gets them thinking about you in a positive light.
5. Resolve reservations and objections through sales skills.
6. Sell them the solution.
7. Finally, use a well-planned follow-up program to make sure they are satisfied, their problems are solved, and they will refer others to you.

STATING YOUR STRATEGY

Using the seven steps as an outline and applying the information about your business and your customers that you've gathered, you can write a succinct marketing strategy. Ideally, it should be concise, fitting into a few sentences—in more complex businesses, a few paragraphs. Any longer description indicates that you are not finished with your homework or that you're trying to cover too much territory. Keep it simple—so simple that you can reel it off at will when anyone asks what you do. Let's look at how this seemingly tough task can work.

Examples

I'll start with a strategy statement for a business I own: a recording studio and audio production company:

> We provide high quality audio recording and sound design to musicians, composers, and commercial clients in upstate New York. Our clients have a need for compelling, high-quality audio recording for presentations and multimedia and music projects at a reasonable rate. We reach them through direct response media, word of mouth, and networking, enhanced by a growing reputation and frequent publicity. Our work is our best advertisement, and we demonstrate it at every chance. Once clients work with us, we work with them on an ongoing basis to promote their projects and help with planning, and we refer others to them whenever possible. We also use an effective incentive program to encourage referrals.

While this is a little long-winded, it is for internal reference only. It gives us a framework for making all our advertising and marketing decisions. When an account rep from a local entertainment magazine pitches us an ad buy, we know the criteria it must satisfy to fit in with our plans. We've defined our market and what we want to accomplish, and we can look at the magazine and decide if it fits in before we spend dollars on expensive ads.

You'll notice that this strategy has something in common with the much-ballyhooed "mission statement" many companies use to motivate their troops. A good mission statement is no more than a well-defined strategy. However, this strategy is marketing specific, that is, it is a model for bringing in and sustaining business, not an overall philosophy. Let's look at another example. How about a freelance business planning consultant:

> I help the owners of new and growing companies write realistic business plans designed to plan growth, encourage capital investment, and, perhaps most important, guide them into the future. Ninety-five percent of my clients come from referrals, which I actively pursue through association membership, business relationships, and my many contacts in the venture capital and banking communities.

This statement keeps the business planner focused on her strengths and the solutions her services offer—including money, organization, and a sense of vision.

She states clearly that the vast majority of her work comes from personal referrals generated through the building of ongoing relationships with people who are likely to encounter her potential clients, the owners of growing businesses.

Tactical Strategies

In military planning, tactics are the tools used to put the overall strategic plan into action. As tools, tactics may have a limited scope and specific use. For example, the business planner may use a limited amount of publicity as a tactic to enhance her reputation. This could involve sending out a press release announcing that XXX Company has retained her for expansion planning (taking this step only with XXX Company's permission, of course). The tactic may only generate a small mention in relevant business publications, but that mention becomes one more proof of her ability and legitimacy in the minds of potential clients who see it. Or it may have been placed to get the attention of a specific person she is seeking to do business with, a person she knows follows the business news. In this case, her tactic, publicity, has a very specific goal in mind. This same approach is often used by corporate headhunters seeking to flush out a specific person they think may be unofficially in the job market. They will run a help wanted ad aimed at that individual's exact qualifications in the hope of making contact.

A strong marketing plan layers tactics to reinforce and enhance their effectiveness. An example would be to run a brief ad in the same publication that prints a story of her new-business planning services. The ad could be as simple as a quote from the CEO of a client company mentioning why he or she feels good about developing a business relationship with her. The combination of good press and an ad starts a process in the readers' minds that will eventually help bring in business. This process uses the power of synergy and the power of repetition to achieve first recognition and then desire.

Synergy, Repetition, and Multiple Contacts

Synergy can be defined as the sum of the parts being greater than expected. It is similar to the way interest builds up on an investment. In marketing, you plan a series of contacts with your customers that eventually make you familiar and respected. Each contact is a step on the ladder to recognition, trust, and finally action. This is where repetition comes in. Say it once, few notice; say it again and again in various interesting and compelling ways, and more people notice. Say it regularly and consistently, and you begin to build trust and confidence in your abilities. Only after repeated contacts (experts estimate it requires 10 to 30) will your marketing have the effect you desire—action on the part of your customers. This means you must commit to an ongoing series of marketing tactics, working in concert, before you will see real results.

One-Shots Don't Work

When I worked in advertising and had introductory meetings with small business owners, I often heard the same complaint: "We tried running an ad; it was expensive and it didn't even pay for itself." This experience generally came as a result of an advertising space salesperson convincing someone to run an ad that was too expensive, in the wrong medium, and probably poorly designed, usually by the media company's in-house staff. The big ad appeared, no one responded, and that was it. The business owners had used up their budget, and the whole experience left a bad taste in their mouths.

The moral of this story is that one-shot marketing does not work. You cannot appear out of a vacuum, shout to the multitudes that you are there, and then crawl back into your office and wait for a response. No one cares and no one will take a chance on this strange creature who popped up one day, attracted their attention, and then disappeared into the ether. Marketing is a series of actions that continues relentlessly, forever.

Failed ads aren't the only one-shots. A booth at a trade show can be a big investment in money, time, and energy yet yield poor results if you don't start with pre-show mailings and calls, practice your best sales skills throughout the show, distribute compelling and informative marketing materials, and follow up relentlessly afterward with the contacts you make. Without this overall strategic approach, a trade show becomes an expensive exercise in futility. With an overall plan, it can be the cornerstone of an entire year's marketing for a self-employed businessperson.

Implementing Your Strategy

Read this book through and then go back and start assembling a strategy based on what you've learned and experienced. Keep it simple, aim at a tightly focused target group of high-quality customers, and plan a relentless and compelling ongoing conversation with them about their needs and your solutions. Get a planning calendar and write in your marketing actions and tactics on specific dates for the entire year ahead. Estimate the costs involved in both time and money and create a simple budget. Then look at your calendar and take the first step on the day and time you've chosen. Keep all the marketing appointments on this calendar and don't put marketing actions aside when you get busy. You're always marketing for sales that are months or even years away.

The One-Sentence Description as a Strategy Model

In this chapter on strategy, I'm going to look again at one tactic that is essential to the success of any business and is especially important for self-employed people. It is strategic in the sense that often defines the message, feeling, and style of the rest of your marketing. I'm speaking of the dreaded *one-sentence description* that we looked at in Chapter 4.

It works like this: You're at a dinner party with a number of people you have just met. Naturally, somebody asks how you make a living. If you're like most of us, you say you're self-employed as a whatever-it-is. The person either shows interest or changes the subject, usually based on their own interest in being self-employed. You've missed a marketing opportunity that only lasted a second. You'll miss this opportunity every time this conversation occurs, whether you're on a plane, at a worksite, or speaking on the phone, all because you didn't have a compelling, clear, succinct description of your business right on the tip of your tongue.

I learned the power of planning your response in these situations when I first played in an original rock band. We were constantly asked what kind of music we did. The answer often determined whether that person came to see the band, wrote about us, or told others about us. The four of us had a hard time coming up with an answer that would achieve those goals—but once we did, we used it all the time. We got a kick out of how music writers would quote it almost word for word in articles, sometimes as a headline! It became the basis of our press kit and helped to build the following we needed to get attention from record companies, radio stations, and music magazines. Now, when I work with bands, I always ask them to come up with a one-sentence description of their music.

Once you've distilled everything you do into one sentence (an almost Zen-like challenge), use that sentence as the basis for the message you put in ads, press releases, sales presentations and any other contact with potential customers. Here are some tips for creating your one-sentence description:

■ *Imagine that you are speaking to an individual who doesn't know you or anything about your business.* Picture that person in front of you, interested and friendly. Use words that you'd use in conversation, not business-speak (please throw away all business language books you may have on your shelf now).

■ *Stress solutions rather than how wonderful and skilled you are.* Understate and be modest; it's much more impressive.

■ *Try to emphasize something interesting about your work.* You want to appeal even to a person with no knowledge of your business. Keep it amusing or informative.

■ *Pick one strength to emphasize.* A writer might say that he or she specializes in clearly explaining complex subjects. Writers would do better to mention a specific specialty like technical writing or medical writing or that they are novelists. Even fiction has many categories.

You might write speculative fiction, romance, mystery, or some other special field.

Choosing a one-sentence description is a challenging task—and one that evolves as your business evolves. You're not boxed in by the description because, if it works well, it will lead to further conversation and interest. It really serves the same purpose as a headline in an ad or press release, drawing attention and leading into the full message of your marketing. In fact, it often resembles your overall business strategy.

Evolving a simple description of a business into a full-blown marketing strategy might not work for a big business—but it can work well for a self-employed person. Simply take that description and turn it around by telling what you do, how you do it, and who you will do it for. Then add a basic description of how you will reach those people and what tactics you'll use. The end result is a basic guide for your marketing that helps you keep on track. If things get slow or don't seem to be working, look at your strategy and make sure you're covering all the whos, whats, and whys. If you're not, address those areas with a renewed effort.

EVOLVING YOUR STRATEGIC APPROACH

In the last paragraph, we mentioned the evolution of your business. All enterprises in life are fluid; your business is no exception. We live in a period of accelerated change; in fact, change may be the basic nature of the environment we live in. The work you do must react and respond to changing conditions if you want to thrive. Adaptability is a basic business skill, and it affects everything about the way you market yourself. The strategy you start with will not be the one you follow a year from now, nor should it be. Strategic thinking is fluid, following the path of least resistance. It is not necessary for the path to be difficult or complex to be successful. The decision to become the master of our own destiny often comes about because of dissatisfaction with how others are doing things and the belief that you can do a better job.

Simplicity is the essence of strategy. The more complex your objectives and your chosen methods of achieving them, the more room there is for errors, un-expected problems, and barriers. Keep it simple and highly focused. You'll find that even a simple target gets more and more complex as you approach it and zero in on the details that make it achievable.

CHAPTER 7

PUTTING YOUR PLAN ON PAPER

In this planning section of *Marketing for the Self-Employed,* I've walked through the basics of marketing a business that is personal to the business owner. The personal nature of your business is important when planning any aspect of your work as a self-employed person, and particularly when you are planning your marketing. You are intimately involved in every aspect of your business from opening the doors in the morning to turning off the lights at night, even if this involves no more than a closet and a lamp over a desk in a corner of your home. Your marketing should be a reflection of your personality because your personal abilities are what your customers want. They want you, not some big company—and they expect marketing that sells you and your own unique abilities.

93

Because of the personal nature of being self-employed, I started out by asking you to consider what you want out of your business, in the context of your whole life. This goal–setting process helps set the overall tone that guides your marketing. Goals are also the place to start your marketing plan.

PUT IT IN WRITING

In this chapter, I'm going to walk you through the actual writing of your personal/business marketing plan. We've looked the basic elements and knowledge you need to get started, including goals, products, customers, targeting, strategy, and tactics. Section Two will cover tactics in detail. Section Three will mirror the third section of your plan, covering money, time, and follow–up. We wrap things up with a walk into the future.

Now we can start writing a plan. It's vital to put your plans down on paper (or on your hard drive) in an organized fashion. Action is the key to successful marketing—and writing a plan is an action that gets you started. The outline in this chapter is comprehensive. It contains many tools you may or may not want to use. After you read through the tactics in Section Two, you'll have a clearer idea of which parts of the outline are relevant to your plan. Leave out the others or put in a note covering ways you might use those parts in the future.

Having a written marketing plan is valuable in a number of ways. It organizes a subject that can be confusing. It sets a timetable of actions that you can follow to get things done without spending all your time searching for business. It gives you a realistic idea of what things will cost you and helps you set priorities for what must happen and what is optional. The finished plan will become an invaluable part of a document package designed to convince banks, other financing sources, or local business development resources to work with you. It shows that you really understand what you do, who requires your services, and how much business volume they can generate. A marketing plan can also help you generate and justify financial projections when applying for loans or grants.

All these considerations are good reasons for putting your plan in writing, organizing it, and printing out copies in a format that others can read and understand. Once you've done so, you might consider running it by a few trusted friends who own businesses or have marketing smarts. Their outside viewpoint can provide invaluable perspective and insight on subjects you may be too close to. Once the plan is in hard copy form (printed out on paper), set it aside for a few days and then read it through to gain another perspective. There's nothing like a finished document to bring the whole picture into view. By then, I hope you'll already be at work making that plan work for you.

MARKETING PLAN OUTLINE

This outline covers far more than you probably need to include in your plan. In particular, the tactics section offers a veritable smorgasbord of ideas, tools, gimmicks, and actions you can use to generate business. This list gives you an overview of the tactics we'll look at more closely in the chapters to come. For now, just start thinking about how they may work for you. Once you have written the other parts of the plan, particularly the goals, product, customer, and strategy sections, you'll have a better idea about which tactics are right for you.

Introduction and Goals

This section is a brief description of what you hope to accomplish with your plan. It should contain specific sales targets in both annual income and in terms of the number and type of new customers you will add to your list of current and past customers. It should also briefly tell how you are integrating your business into other relevant areas of your life and define any new products or services you plan to introduce in the next year. Brevity is important because you'll go over these items in detail later.

Description of Business

State what you do, sell, or solve, and any specific products or services you offer from a marketing point of view. That is, don't just list them, say why anyone would want to purchase them. List the skills, packaging, proprietary trademarks, or technology you offer, any unusual experience you can leverage into sales, and so on. This is your stock in trade, that is, what you have to offer your customers.

Description of Customers and Markets

List who will buy from you and why, who and what they are, where they are, what dollar volume they spend on your services, and what potential new markets you can sell to. This outlines the demographics of your customer base. Arrange the list in order of priority, best potential customers first.

Strategy for Reaching Your Target Markets

Describe how you will reach out to your potential, current, and past customers, tell them about the solutions you offer, sell them on those solutions, generate referral business, and use follow-up to generate additional sales. This is a communications strategy, first and foremost. As such, it should focus on developing a clear and compelling message that resonates with the needs and desires of your customers. Then you will develop a tactical plan to reach them and communicate with them.

Tactics to Implement Your Strategy

Tactics are tools like advertising, publicity, sales skills, networking, the way you present yourself, and the many other communications tools used by successful marketers. Your plan should consist of several tactics that overlap, convey a consistent message, and reinforce each other in a positive way. These tactics include:

- Identity elements—name, tagline, logo
- Marketing and contact information—brochures, business cards, stationery, sales letters, newsletters, Web sites
- Direct response marketing—direct mail, telemarketing, seminars
- Advertising—print, TV, and radio messages
- Telephone—cold calling, information surveys, general phone manner
- Publicity—news releases, articles, expert-source quotes
- Networking—trade shows and association memberships
- Sales—developing sales skills and practicing them constantly
- Follow-up—finding out how customers regard the work, developing an active referral network

Each of these tactics gets detailed coverage in its own chapter in Section Two.

In your plan, briefly explain how you'll use the tactic. For instance, under Publicity you might write: "I will develop a media list, write and send out press releases telling about interesting and newsworthy developments in my business area, write articles for publication, accept public speaking engagements, teach one basic no-cost seminar every six months at a local business group, and join three associations my customers are likely to join. I will also position myself as an expert in my profession by developing personal contacts in the professional media and positioning myself as a useful resource on the subjects I specialize in."

While your publicity aspirations may not be this complex, your plan should at least address the basic possibilities of each tactic and attempt to put them into your budget and calendar. Planning is an ongoing process; you may find that things that seem hard now may become easier in the future as you gain experience. Eliminating any potential tools at this point may severely limit you later.

Budgets

Your plan should include a projected budget for all of your efforts. While this may be difficult to compile now, you can make estimates, place them into a calendar, and then get an idea of how much all of this costs over a year's time. From that projection you can determine which tactics will be most cost effective and where you can gradually introduce new ones. Again there is no rule as to how much to spend—although, if well planned, more spending should result in more profitable business.

If you have very limited resources now, plan on using inexpensive tactics like telephone prospecting, networking, and publicity and gradually work in more expensive tactics as your cash flow increases. It helps to shoot for an overall percentage of sales as a marketing figure, perhaps 10 percent. Chapter 8 covers budgeting in more detail.

Marketing Calendar

Time is the other major resource required for effective marketing. It takes a lot of time to get a marketing plan organized and written and to implement it during the period it covers. The most efficient way to organize your marketing time is to use a planner or a planning calendar to keep your marketing on track. This is particularly important because marketing requires time to take effect. When we get busy, most of us tend to put our marketing work on the back burner. An unfortunate side effect of this can be a roller coaster of busy versus slow times. Remember, your marketing always aims to generate future business. Stop marketing when you're busy and you may suddenly find yourself twiddling your thumbs and watching the bills stack up.

There are many good planners on the market, each with its own system for use. I highly recommend buying one and learning how to use it. Often the publishers offer seminars on time management. It is money well spent. Take your planner and fill in your marketing actions for the next year, using the suggestions in Chapter 21. I find that it helps me to have a 12-month, erasable wall calendar in my office with each action clearly in front of me. You can also use your calendar or planner to put together spending projections ahead of time so that you can set aside money for future marketing actions.

LOOK AHEAD

The final component of your marketing plan is the future. Plans are not written in stone; like goals, they are guidelines that you adapt and change as you acquire experience or the desire to go in a different direction. End your plan with a little free association about possible directions your marketing and business may take once you're established. Those directions will help you guide your business into the future and cope with the rapid pace of change we live with.

CHAPTER 8

MONEY, TIME,
AND MARKETING

Money is the primary problem most self-employed people encounter when it comes to marketing themselves. Time is the second concern. Because the two are so intertwined, I'll deal with both of them in this chapter. We're going to look at the value of your time in terms of dollars and cents and how that value works when you spend it on marketing. First let's look at an example that makes this all a little less confusing.

Joe is an electrician who usually bills by the hour for his work. His rate is $50 per hour and he justifies it by offering licensed, skilled, dependable, and safe work. He gets the job done and done right the first time. Joe listens to his commercial customers during the small-talk sessions that accompany every job and starts hearing that there is a real need for someone like him who understands and installs the wiring for computer networks. The market is wide open, particularly in the small to medium-size business market he serves. He decides to specialize in network installation and service.

Assuming Joe has learned the skills and accumulated the knowledge he needs to perform these services, his biggest challenge is to tell the world—or at least his established customers—about his new product. Recognizing this, he decides to write a simple marketing plan. His plan includes putting together a brochure, combining it with a sales letter, sending it to a list of current and potential customers, and simultaneously beginning to run a small display ad in his area business newspaper. He'll call every past and present customer after the letters go out and then start calling the most likely prospects on the list of potential customers he will be using.

The plan is simple. To put it into action, he must first produce the brochure, letter, and ad, assemble a mailing and phone list, and send out the packages. At this point he has two choices. He can write up some text and have a friend use a personal computer to put together a brochure, let the publication running the ad do the design for it (something they offer at a very low price as part of the media buy), and sit at his kitchen table licking envelopes and sticking stamps. Alternatively, he can hire a small advertising design agency with an experienced copywriter to handle the brochure copy, design, and printing, as well as the ad layout. He can also call a mailing shop and arrange to have them print out personalized versions of the sales letter from an industry-specific list he rents, mechanically address and stuff the envelopes, and do the mailing for him.

The decision depends on time and money—and the most effective allocation of these limited resources. The design agency and the letter shop will charge him around $50 an hour for their work. His friend will put together the brochure on the side for a couple of hundred dollars total—but that means Joe will be spend-ing his time trying to write copy, deal with printers, stick stamps and, on top of these tasks, make calls and do his work.

Going with the pros will cost Joe several thousand dollars. The ads will be compelling and will stand out when compared to the other ads in the publication, many of which will have been put together under pres-sure by a low-paid staff designer. The brochure and the ads will feature a unified message that directly addresses the problems that Joe's potential customers face. The brochure will look professional and will assure the customers that they are dealing with an established computer installation company rather than a fly-by-night outfit set up in someone's spare bedroom. (Joe does work out of a spare room, but that's not a market-ing point!) The letter shop mailing will go to a highly targeted list based on Joe's description of his ideal cus-tomers and the experience of the list broker. Instead of a form letter, each of these customers (information systems professionals) will get a personalized, professionally written letter from Joe introducing himself, identifying a problem they all are dealing with daily, and offering a solution.

The low-budget route costs Joe about a thousand dollars plus the ad buy. It also requires many hours of his time writing and rewriting, fixing his friend's mistakes, accumulating names for his list, dealing with the confusing demands of printers, media salespeople, and the post office, and several late nights filling envelopes. In spite of his best efforts, Joe is not an experienced writer and his message meanders, emphasizing buzzwords like quality and service without directly dealing with the actual problems his customers face. The brochure looks cheap and has no effective headline or call to action. The packages go out, often addressed to an anonymous Information Systems Manager because Joe couldn't get specific names. When it comes to follow-up calls, Joe still doesn't have names so he gets blown off by gatekeepers when he tries to call.

In deciding which scenario he should follow, Joe probably wouldn't have the luxury of knowing how things will turn out. Instead he will be looking at the bottom line of how much it all costs. The do-it-yourself approach is attractive at the outset because the savings are apparent and they are significant. The hiring-the-pros approach seems exorbitant for a one-person business. This is the point where most of us would make a big mistake based on misconceptions about money, time, and marketing. Marketing is not a place to save money; it is a place to invest money for a significant return.

Understanding that marketing is an investment rather than an expense is vital when deciding how much to spend and where. Typically, it is better to invest more in your marketing—where it can build your business—than it is to spend money on other expenses that merely keep you going. Marketing is not the place to pinch pennies; it is the place to put extra cash that you want to see grow and compound.

In Joe's case, time and skill are major factors. Is he better off spending his $50/hour time stuffing envelopes and not getting paid or focusing on paying work and hiring others to do what they do well? The obvious answer is that Joe should twist wires for $50 an hour and pay the designers and other pros their $50 to create really powerful marketing tools for his business. If you are good at what you do, then you should seek out others who excel at the things you don't know and use their skills.

At first glance, this looks like an even trade-off: Joe goes back to his work at $50 an hour and turns around and pays others the same to work on his marketing tools. But by forgoing the income, Joe essentially winds up paying an untrained amateur—himself—to do work that he could get done by experts for the same price. Not only that, but the professional marketing will be so much more effective that he'll get better, more lucrative work as a result. Even when he goes to make follow-up calls (a job he must do himself), he'll find a much more receptive audience because his marketing did a better job of communicating what he offers.

This scenario is the same for all self-employed people. We are specialists. We cannot know and do everything, nor do we want to. You might spend hours struggling to write a letter that an experienced copywriter could put together much faster. They know what questions to ask about your business and your customers, how to quickly digest that information and then choose the most effective message it contains. They know how to strip away superfluous content and get to the point. This can be said of any experienced specialist including you, whether you're a dog groomer or an attorney. And the even $50 in this example just simplifies the discussion; you can benefit from hiring services even when they cost more per hour than what you charge for your own work, if what you get takes fewer hours or is more valuable than what you can do for yourself.

SCARCITY MENTALITY

In spite of this clear benefit, I have had repeated experiences with self-employed people who suffer from what I call a *scarcity mentality.* They'll do anything to avoid spending a buck today for a result tomorrow. The excuses are legion:

- "I'm the only one who really knows my market."
- "Anyone can write [design, sell, whatever] that sort of stuff."
- "Things are slow, and I just don't have the money."
- "No one cares what things look like as long as you do a good job."

These justifications for not spending money are extremely dangerous ways to think about your business. Marketing requires just as much long-term commitment as the original decision you made to go into business. That commitment means money and time and energy combined with creativity. You can replace any of these ingredients you lack by using others effectively. If you don't have money, be prepared to spend time and pull out the stops creatively. You'll need to develop a plan that emphasizes personal contact, publicity, networking, and other time-consuming but relatively inexpensive tactics. If you have money but no time and little creative interest, hire others and learn from them as they work with you.

FINDING MONEY FOR MARKETING YOURSELF

It is a fortunate paradox that when you have time you usually are short of money and vice versa. It's fortunate because this feast-and-famine cycle offers a way to break out of itself. If your work is slow, you've got the time to devote to marketing. That means choosing a strategy and tactics that require your personal action instead of large sums of money. Once the work comes in and you are busy, you have the money to hand off some of your marketing to others, using tactics that require less personal involvement. If you get it right, you'll eventually find an equilibrium point where you have an established budget in both time and money for your marketing and a steady stream of work.

How much money is enough? The answer is: It depends. A freelance writer doesn't really need a big marketing budget. She might subscribe to several magazines, join several online services, research article ideas, and work on reselling existing articles. However, she will invest considerable time in querying editors, doing research, developing ideas on spec, and sending out articles or book proposals.

On the other hand, the owner of a gift shop may have a much different set of financial needs when it comes to marketing. She'll run ads every week in the local paper, do newsletter mailings monthly to her customer list, maintain a Web site featuring new products, and regularly update her displays and signage. These things all require cash money on a regular basis and are a regular part of her monthly overhead. Because she must spend the majority of her time on running the shop and buying merchandise, she may hire a small agency to handle most of these tasks for her.

Your own budget will come out of the needs of your business. Each tactic in Section Two has guidelines about how much it may cost in both time and money. These are part of the criteria you'll use in choosing which tactics will work for your business. Once you've decided on a set of interlocking actions (tactics), you'll need to put together a budget and calendar for implementing them. Make sure you consider the cost in both time and money. The two are interrelated and cannot be separated. Let's look at how you can effectively allocate your time and money to get the results you want.

Your Budget

One of the important lessons you'll learn as you market yourself is that it is an incremental process. You take step after step and eventually reach your goals. Financially, this means that you must allocate your resources in increments rather than throwing one lump sum at your promotional efforts. Once you've covered some of your marketing start-up costs like business cards and brochures, you should put a percentage of your income aside monthly for marketing yourself. By considering it a part of your monthly overhead that must be paid as a regular expense, you'll start to market yourself regularly and consistently.

The percentage you set aside will be based on what works for your business. The gift shop owner in the example above might dedicate 5 percent to 10 percent of her total sales for advertising and other ongoing marketing. The freelance writer might only allocate a small sum for postage, calls, and copies.

Besides the dollars, you must also allocate a specific amount of time, on a regular basis, dedicated to marketing yourself. When I took piano lessons in college, my teacher taught me a valuable lesson about time and practice. I'd skip my half-hour practice for several days and then try to make it up by doing a marathon session before my lesson. She always knew. Her prescription and rule was that it is much more valuable to devote 15 minutes every day to something than to spend two hours once a week. The daily exposure builds your skill level on a subconscious basis by keeping you in ongoing contact with your practice. Skipping five days and plunging in often means starting over every week.

Your personal involvement in marketing will be much more effective if you budget a certain amount of time daily to your marketing. As little as 15 minutes per day five days a week adds up fast. In a year, you'll spend about 60 hours on marketing, the equivalent of two solid weeks of work. These 15 minutes are highly leveraged time. If you spend them calling potential customers and make one contact per week that generates $200 worth of profits, you're making over $160 per hour for your efforts—not bad by any criterion. It's easy to play this game as a motivational method. For instance, suppose you send out five sales letters per day, resulting in that profit of $200 per week. Those 25 weekly letters are worth $8 each! Knowing that every letter you send, successful or not, is worth $8 can be an excellent motivator.

Motivation is another important part of scheduling regular daily marketing activities. It is easier to motivate yourself to complete a short but effective task each day than to gear up to tackle a big project every couple of weeks. One of the secrets of achieving any goal is to build in simple victories along the way, victories that keep you interested and positive about your marketing. If your time is spent on mailings, as in the previous example, your victory may be just getting those five envelopes into the mail each day, whether they generate responses or not.

Effective budgeting and scheduling has a lot to do with motivation. As a self-employed person, you probably miss the camaraderie that helps a group stay on track during a project. You must create structures that make it easy to keep yourself on track without having others to cheer you on. Those structures are budgets, goals, and calendars—and they are all interrelated.

You may set a goal for the next year, based on the standards we looked at in Chapter 2. To achieve that goal, you break it down into steps or tasks that must be accomplished to reach it. Once you've broken your marketing goal down into steps, based on the information you acquire about your business and customers and your plan, you assign those steps to specific dates on your calendar. These dates or deadlines are targets that keep you making progress. Once you've assigned deadlines, you go back and estimate costs involved in both time and money and adjust your target dates. This adjustment will be based on how much money you have to spend at a given time and how much time the task requires.

Scheduling and budgeting is an ongoing process just like marketing. Your goals and resources will change. Your priorities will change. Knowledge and skill you acquire may shorten or eliminate some steps. Once you set up a plan and a calendar, you enter the process of marketing itself, which is an organic and fluid experience. Like all natural series of events, it has no definable finish point. It is an integral part of being self-employed.

The Costs of Marketing

Because prices change constantly and each self-employed business, location, and market have different needs, I cannot offer specific dollar estimates for your marketing. And if I did, they would only serve as extremely loose guidelines. You have to do some homework yourself to assemble a marketing budget. Because you work from a plan (and here's a good reason to do so) you have a reference to work from when figuring out a budget. Take your ideal plan and break it down into actions (as we discussed earlier) and assign a cost in both time and money to each action.

For example, consider the cost of running an ad every two weeks in a local publication. Your start-up costs will include production and films for the printer, and you may have to put up a few weeks' worth of payments in advance. You will also spend time with a media salesperson, a writer, and a graphic designer, and time making calls to assure that things continue as you wish. This includes any changes in ad content, size, location, and frequency. You'll spend more time at the outset than later on, but you should be able to project your actual cost, on a monthly basis, to maintain the ad. As soon as you have that monthly number, you can add it to your overhead and allocate funds for it every month just as you do when you pay your other bills.

The idea is to get your marketing up and running and never let it stop. You'll fine-tune here and there, adding and changing things as you determine how well they work, but you'll always be marketing. It should just be another of those things you do to run your business. The effects of these expenditures won't be instant, but eventually they will yield steady results.

Your Business as a Machine

Many entrepreneurs like to think of themselves as free spirits, going with the flow and acting as the situation warrants. While this works well during the unpredictable start-up phase of a new business, it does not work well for day-to-day operations, a primary reason why many well-known entrepreneurs lose their grip after their companies reach a more mature stage. In my experience, being self-employed has little to do with being an entrepreneur and a lot to do with running or managing an established enterprise. We don't set out to build a company; we set out to make a good living on our own terms.

Continual entrepreneurship is the cause of much of the feast-or-famine nature of being self-employed. Each time we complete a job for a customer we reinvent the wheel, starting over again to find more work. From a marketing perspective, this is an inefficient way to work. Fortunately, there is a better model for small business success than the entrepreneurial one touted in small business magazines. It's based on the reason popular franchises work for their owners.

Franchise buyers aren't seeking entrepreneurial opportunities; they want a turnkey business they can purchase, learn to run (with organized training to make the process efficient), and make a living out of from day one. So they buy a franchise, which is in essence a business machine rather than a start-up. Theoretically, it is a proven system. While the reality of franchise ownership seldom lives up to the promise, there are several things a self-employed person can learn from the franchise model.

First, it pays to automate as many of your regular actions as possible. Most of us have to pay our overhead bills monthly, which is a form of automation. If you take it a step further and analyze any regular business actions you take, you'll find that by creating a system based on a calendar you can get a lot more done. Planning a year of marketing actions down to the daily things like customer meetings and contacts means that you have a system for marketing yourself—a marketing machine working constantly to bring you business. And turning your marketing into a system has some distinct advantages.

First, it is predictable. You'll get to know any seasonal changes; you'll recognize natural slow and fast periods as opposed to unexpected slow periods that are warning signs. You'll know how much money you'll be spending and have a better idea how much you'll make. And after a few years, you'll have documented proof that your system works, something that will make it much easier to get credit to buy a home or expand your business.

Second, the marketing system takes care of itself, ticking along to keep work coming in rain or shine, recession or expansion. It becomes an information system, telling you about what you do, ways you can improve your business, what your customers want, and ways you can increase your income with new products or services. The information comes from regular customer contact and feedback from those customers. Being organized and systematic not only saves money, it saves time—and having enough of both is a sign of successful marketing.

TACTICS: THE TOOLS OF THE TRADE

CHAPTER 9

YOUR IDENTITY IN
THE MARKETPLACE

McDonald's. Coke. Kodak. Dean Witter. Recognize any of them? Of course you do. And as you think of each, you probably think about golden arches, red cans, yellow film boxes, and that warm voice talking about listening to the client. These companies have an extremely strong identity in our culture, an identity built over many years and with the investment of millions of dollars and the creative efforts of thousands of highly trained people. The identities of these powerful companies are valuable assets they must protect and nurture constantly to maintain their effectiveness as marketing tools.

Each of these companies started with an individual with a unique marketing vision. George Eastman chose the word Kodak because it meant nothing, it was unique, and it was easy to remember and pronounce. It was a clean slate to build an internationally recognized trademark on.

McDonald's is a homey sounding business name, easy to remember and all-American. Dean Witter sounds like a knowledgeable, highly professional elder statesman of finance, someone you'd trust with your future. Coca-Cola is catchy, alliterative, memorable, and descriptive. Paired with its distinctive bottle shape and an evolving series of logos in red and white, it has impressed itself into our planet's culture.

Your name and the way you present it is equally important to the success of your business. Often it represents that vital first impression that colors much of a customer's future view of your business. It can mean the difference between a customer accepting and trusting you or deciding immediately that they are not interested. If your name is difficult to remember or pronounce, it will cost you business every day.

You'll be investing all of your time and all of your money in your business identity. Each success will increase its value and each mistake or misstep will take a little away. Because you have such a heavy investment in the power of your name, it is important to get it right early in your marketing process. That's why your identity is the first marketing tactic we're looking at. So what is it?

It starts with your business or company name. It may simply be your own name followed by a brief description or *tagline* that further defines what you do. In certain cases you'll want to have at least the guise of a company name—even if the company is nothing more than you working in a spare room. We'll look at when and why choosing a "doing business as" (DBA) name is the right move.

Do people easily remember your name the first time you say it? Or do they stumble and often ask you to repeat it? Is it easy to spell and pronounce? Have you done business successfully under your name up till now? If your name is easy to pronounce, spell, and remember, then it is fine to use it as a business identifier. If it is hard to pronounce, potential customers may hesitate to call because of embarrassment at mispronouncing your name. Worse, they will misspell or forget it, making it difficult to find you when they want to. You should consider choosing a company name. This also gives you the opportunity to choose a name that tells something about the services and products you offer.

Choosing a new business name is a real challenge. Something over 20 million new businesses start up in the United States alone each year. Creating a unique, descriptive, protectable name is almost impossible. Name consultants charge large fees to generate lists of names using creative techniques like brainstorming and exotic techniques involving computer programs that generate meaningless words (like Kodak). Often they will generate thousands of names before arriving at one that satisfies all the requirements. And, equally often, they will fail to find the right name.

Your search for a great business name need not be so complex unless you are building a national brand. The average self-employed person does business within a very limited sphere. The name they choose does not have to be totally unique because they probably will never face a challenge from someone with the same name. However, you should attempt to come up with an original name for a number of reasons. They include:

■ *You can apply for a trademark.* Registered trademark status means that you can protect your business name from use by others in your state or nationally, depending on how far your registration goes. To qualify for registration, your name must be unique and nondescriptive. Unusual spellings of common words are not considered unique. Normal descriptive names like Good Pizza Company may not pass muster, either. Getting a trademark requires the help of an attorney with intellectual property law experience.

■ *You can increase the value of your business.* If you own a trademark for a company or product name, then it becomes an asset you can invest money in. Should you sell your business, a recognized trade name may increase the value of your company.

■ *You can help people remember you.* For the average self-employed person, this is the number one reason for carefully selecting your business name. Because word-of-mouth publicity and other personal marketing tools are so important to a self-employed person, you need a name that sticks in people's minds after one or two exposures. This saves you money because it means that you need fewer contacts to make an impression.

■ *You can help define how you do business.* If you're in a goofy business, you can choose a goofy or clever name—otherwise, play it straight. Many times you'll want a name that conveys solid reliability, technical expertise, or a cutting-edge attitude. Match the name to the type of business you are in. An accountant will probably want a conservative name, while a multimedia developer may choose something hi-tech and trendy.

■ *You can make yourself known on a national scale.* Jo-Mar's Grocery is fine for a mom and pop store. However, mom and pop stores are on the way out because they cannot expand their sphere of influence unless they develop a special product that can reach a bigger market. It's no different for any small business. With e-mail and the proliferation of the Internet, fax machines, and teleconferencing, you may find yourself doing business all over the country and possibly the world. Choosing a good name will help you stand out across the country as well as across the street.

■ *You can avoid limiting yourself.* Otherwise, you might go from Cal's Worms and Live Bait to Cal's Bait and Tackle to Cal's Fishing World and Marina to Cal's Sporting Life. Actually, if Cal just started out with Cal's and used a tagline to delineate his business he could always upgrade by changing his tagline.

Taglines

Taglines are the second component of your identity. Like the one-sentence description I asked you to come up with in Chapter 4, a tagline expands on your name with a compelling detail about your business. Cal's, The Place for Bait That Pulls Them In. Cal's, Everything for the In-Fisherman. Cal's, the Area's Fishing One-Stop. Cal's, Everything for Sports People, Worldwide.

Taglines have the advantage of flexibility. You can choose a memorable yet generic name and use a tagline to tell what you do. You can adapt the tagline to incorporate changes and develop different taglines for different markets. My company was Edic Wells Associates, Business Writing and Market Planning. I've since changed my tagline to Multimedia Communications because of a change in focus. Edic Wells Associates is intentionally generic because my range of interests is changing with the times and I wanted a name that remained stable for my clients even as my business changed.

Taglines also give you a chance to have some fun with your name. Esperanto's Pizza gains a lot of attitude when you add a few words. Esperanto's Pizza, Thatsa

Lotta Pie! gives them a hook to use in ads, packaging, and anywhere else. It also lends itself to a logo or visual image that is an important part of their identity.

Logos

Logotypes or logos are visual symbols of your business. They are important because many of us think visually; in other words, we see pictures in our heads when we think of something. By associating a picture with your name, you strengthen the impression you make. Take Esperanto's Pizza. Their logo might show a cartoon character straining under the weight of a huge pizza. Add in "Thatsa Lotta Pie!" and you have a combination of name, picture, and tagline working together to create a memorable impression.

Designing an effective logo is not the job for an amateur. Throwing together some clip art on your computer can work—but clip art is so common nowadays that you run the risk of having a generic logo, defeating the purpose in the first place. I highly recommend using a skilled graphic designer to create your logo. The designer should have many logos in his or her portfolio. Choose one whose work holds up to the logos you've seen for successful companies and products. Such logos are simple and compelling; yours should visually reinforce your name and tagline or profession.

Logo design is expensive, ranging from several hundred to several thousand dollars. You can save money by having your designer set your name in a distinctive typeface rather than drawing a design. This type of logo is usually fine for the average self-employed businessperson. You can always add a picture or symbol later.

Use your name, tagline, and logo consistently. It helps to have the same designer handle all your stationary, including business cards, letterhead, invoices, and so on. This will ensure that you convey a consistent image throughout all your correspondence with your customers. Remember, even an invoice is an opportunity to market yourself. And the more professional it looks, the more likely you are to get paid on time—an added bonus.

PACKAGING

Most self-employed people don't have unique packaging for their products. After all, how do you package a service? The answer is by surrounding the actual service with ads, business cards, follow-up and thank you letters, and other measures that reinforce your identity in the customer's eyes. This packaging will help generate repeat business because, like a compelling box on a shelf, it is attractive and appealing. Ever hear someone described as "having the whole package together"? People like that understand that identity is a system of visual, auditory, and mental symbols that reinforce the personal and professional impression you leave with a potential customer.

Your package combines your name, tagline, logo, color scheme, and personality. For many self-employed people, it consists of a handshake, a meeting, and a business card. For others, packaging is everything from a utilitarian box or bag to a whole range of items emblazoned with clever logos and slogans. Packaging can even generate a profitable product—like those Hard Rock Cafe T-shirts you see everywhere.

If you deal with a lot of customers or have a picturesque name or location, capitalize on it. A friend runs a successful nightclub called The Bug Jar with two partners. Besides the unusual name, they have a tagline (Your Bar On Earth) and a logo featuring a ying-yang symbol. Soon after opening, they had bumper stickers printed featuring all three identity components. They found that they couldn't give them away at the bar because they ended up stuck all over everything. So they put them in a vending machine for 50 cents each. To date, they've gone through 4,500 of them! They also do T-shirts in similar quantities and recently trademarked their name, tagline, and logo to avoid rip-offs.

The smallest business can benefit from a little creativity when it comes to packaging. A gift shop owner has a large rubber stamp made and puts her clerks to work stamping designs on bags when they're not busy. The bags are very popular and though they're free they contribute to sales because they serve as last-minute gift wrap. While pizza parlors can buy generic preprinted boxes, smart pizza makers build identity by splashing their name and logo on the box. How many times have you been at a party and wondered where the pizza came from? No logo, no opportunity to capitalize on that great word of mouth (or taste of mouth) advertising!

Your identity is more than fancy logos and business cards, though. When you get down to it, you must provide really great service, excellent products, and a positive attitude if you hope to succeed. But if you're doing all those things, it can't hurt to be memorable and professional looking, too.

CHAPTER 10

PRODUCING EFFECTIVE PRINT MARKETING MATERIALS

One of the first things most new business owners do is run out and have business cards printed, followed by stationery, and then, if things are going well, a brochure. These print materials are part of what ad agencies call *collateral*, a term for all the various support materials they must generate as part of an ad campaign. These collateral materials can range from postcards to brochures to in-store displays and include almost anything imaginable. For the self-employed person, these marketing materials often supersede or replace advertising and may become a primary means of telling your story.

For most self-employed people, there is a minimum of two pieces you must consider to support all your marketing—business cards and a capability brochure or information sheet telling about the solutions you offer. You need the cards to provide you with an instant way to give people all your contact information in one simple format. The brochures or fact sheets exist to flesh out your one-sentence description, to follow up on personal contacts and responses to ads, and to distribute at events like trade shows and conferences. You can also use them as direct mail pieces, to reinforce a sales presentation, and in many other ways, limited only by your marketing attitude and imagination.

When I talk to small business owners about these marketing materials, my focus is always on how to use them. Unfortunately, their focus is usually on how much they cost to produce. Few of us really enjoy shelling out for writing, design, and printing of brochures. Yet these are effective marketing tools that, if done right, will easily return your investment. The key is to do them right from the beginning.

In this chapter, we'll be looking at how to produce and use print marketing materials. We'll look at the best way to work with copywriters, designers, and printers to get professional, cost-effective marketing materials. Most important, we'll look at how to avoid the common syndrome of having boxes of unused business cards and brochures sitting in a closet until they go stale. Getting these marketing tools out in the world and working for you is essential to their success.

WORKING WITH THE PROS

Because of the advent of inexpensive desktop publishing systems, we see floods of poorly written, poorly designed laser-printed brochures, post cards, and business cards. In spite of the ease of use most desktop publishing software promises, simply owning a computer does not make you into a designer, any more than buying a power saw will turn you into a carpenter. There is a skill and an art involved in producing effective marketing pieces that will bring in profitable, interesting business. Unless you are an experienced designer, writer, and marketing person, I strongly recommend using skilled pros to create your marketing materials. The results will really show how these people earn their money.

Many of the marketing tactics we'll look at in Section Two do not require large sums of money to put into action. Personal sales, telephone contacts, networking, and basic publicity are techniques that rely more on your ability and time than your money. However, for each of these techniques to work well, you need professional-looking support materials to back up your story.

Imagine you make a successful cold call to a prospective client, get an appointment, and make a convincing sales presentation—and then leave behind a generic business card and one of those preprinted brochures that you've run through your laser printer to add some amateur copy about your business. Your new client sits down a few hours later, after the excitement of your sales presentation has worn off, and takes a look at your stuff. With a sinking heart, he starts to think that the person who so convincingly sold him on the benefits of doing business is a cheapskate, or worse, incompetent. Your hard-won sale starts to lose the momentum you worked very hard to generate.

This scenario is common. Instead of supporting your sales presentation, your marketing materials torpedoed it. It is all a part of the process that is a recurring theme throughout this book. Marketing is an ongoing series of contacts that continues until customers decide to buy, that follow up until they buy again, and that follow up further until they recommend you to someone else. Each contact should build on the others to create the synergy that eventually causes your prospect to have enough faith in you to take the plunge and do business. If your marketing tactics fail to support the process, they can result in the entire edifice dissolving into nothing. It's important to get it right.

The arguments for using professionals to produce your marketing materials include:

- *The message will be compelling and consistent.* Everything from ad to postcard to brochure and on through all the rest of your materials will convey the same message.
- *The look will be professional.* This will position you, in your market, as a pro.

- *You'll save money on design.* Things will get done right from the beginning, including proofreading, color separations, printing specs, estimates, and double- and triple-checking of everything.
- *You'll probably save money on printing, too.* Most designers get a break on printing quotes—they buy printing all the time, so they know who the reliable, high-quality printers are and they also know many ways to save money through creative design. A good designer can make a two-color piece look far better than a full-blown four-color piece designed by someone who doesn't understand the process.
- *You'll get better art.* If you need photos or illustrations, a good designer can find high-quality work, either original or stock, that will fit your needs and budget and will reproduce well (unlike your cousin Lennie's snapshots).

So where do you find these miracle workers and how much will it cost? You start by looking for brochures, ads, and business cards that catch your eye, preferably in a field similar to your own. I suggest focusing on small businesses dealing with graphic design firms rather than ad agencies, with two exceptions. If you are going to be buying regular amounts of media advertising, an ad agency may be willing to do business with you. For the most part, even small agencies need media buys in the $50,000-plus range to justify taking on a client. The other exception is for a small business that primarily markets itself via direct response including mail and telemarketing. There are direct response advertising agencies who specialize in this highly targeted and effective marketing. If you contemplate mass mailings or solicitations, you might benefit from the use of direct response experts. (We'll look at direct response in detail in Chapter 12.)

Once you've found a few pieces you like, contact the companies that use them and ask to talk to the owner. Explain that you are a fellow business owner and ask if you can compare notes about their experience producing their brochure (cards, ads, whatever). If they are happy with the people they worked with, they'll recommend them. If the same designer or firm gets mentioned more than once, you have a good candidate. By the way, calling your fellow business owners for information like this is an excellent way to start networking your own business by starting a relationship with other company owners. Even the solitary self-employed person has far more in common with a company owner than a corporate executive. You'll usually find these entrepreneurs more than willing to talk shop with a fellow business owner.

Between this kind of networking and referrals from friends and business associates, you'll probably end up with several names of small graphic design and advertising agencies. These agencies often include a designer, an account executive who generates and maintains business relationships, and possibly a writer. They may have a media buyer or use an outside service. They're small enough to take on a small business—in fact, they are often small business marketing experts.

Call each of them and make an appointment to see their work. Don't feel embarrassed if your office is a spare room. Many of their clients are just like you, and they know from experience that you can't judge the success of a business by its offices. If you don't have a place to meet, go to their place. Look at their portfolio and listen to their pitch. Think about the questions they ask you. Do they indicate an interest in how your business works? Based on what you've learned from this book, does it sound like they are asking marketing-related questions? If they ask about your customers first, it's a good sign.

As you look at their portfolio, notice what they stress. If they dwell on the problems they faced from a design or technical standpoint, they may be a little too focused on their end of things. If they explain the thinking behind each piece and how effective it was, you've got a good prospect. You're looking for more than a designer; you're looking for a partner who will take an active interest in the success of your marketing. After all, if you are successful, you'll provide more business for them.

Their design approach should be flexible and simple to understand. The basic message should go to the heart of the matter and not hide itself in a clutter of design elements or extraneous words. The designer should be flexible, not using the same look for every client, but instead tailoring the look to the buyer or reader. When you see a piece that works well for you, ask about the copywriter who wrote it. Most graphic design firms work regularly with several copywriters and may be able to make a referral. Finding the right writer is another critical step in getting really effective marketing materials.

WRITERS

Writers who use their writing to sell are called *copywriters* and the work they do is called *copy*. This is not to be confused with *copyright,* which is a legal protection for writing. Copywriters are a breed apart from other writers like novelists, article writers, or technical writers. They specialize in writing that explains, compels, and sells. They know how to distill your business into words that speak directly to your customers' interests and needs. In fact, most copywriters picture an imaginary customer and write to them as they write.

While you may find a designer first, you both will need a concept and copy before the designer can get started. Only a designer with a lack of market smarts would try to design without a message to work with. Everything about your marketing materials from design to paper stock to printing should reinforce the writer's message. And that message must do the job or all the rest is for naught.

Good writers aren't cheap—but they will always make you money in the long run. Expect to pay from $25 to $75 an hour for their time. In most cases, you'll want them to quote you one price for a predetermined amount of writing, usually two or three concepts, two drafts, and a final revision. You don't pay by the word for one simple reason: The best copy is often succinct and direct, with no flowery metaphors, long-winded explanations, or other padding. The last thing you want to do is provide an incentive to make it longer!

Good writers will grill you about your business. They'll want to know about your personal style, your competition, and—most important—your customers' needs and desires. Share your marketing plan and any accumulated knowledge you have. Stay open to new ideas they may offer, even about the very core of what you do. In my work as a copywriter, I have often been able to identify completely new markets or new approaches for my clients simply because I have an experienced outside perspective. In many ways, I felt that this was the real value and service I offered my clients.

If possible, invite them to see you in action, working and interacting with your customers. This gives them a chance to pick up on details and color that you take for granted. It also helps them put themselves into the shoes of your prospective customers, offering clues to what will really grab attention. Once they have the information they need and they understand the function of the piece they are writing, let them go and come up with some ideas.

Every effective ad, brochure, and sales letter has the same basic components. There is a headline or *head* that grabs attention by offering a solution or posing a question that addresses a major concern of the readers or startles them into a new perspective. The head is followed by *body copy,* which offers solutions to the customers' problems. It may list features of your business (the bells and whistles) along with benefits to the customers of each feature. This feature-benefit comparison is a classic marketing technique and will show up in your sales presentation and any other place where you explain your business to others.

The body copy may have *subheads* that pull the reader through each section of the piece. Subheads are heads that tell what each paragraph or section of the body copy will cover. They are important because many readers will skim the piece and read only those areas whose subheads draw their interest. There must be an *offer* or invitation to take action somewhere, either in the body copy or the headlines and subheads. Other copy items are *picture captions,* important because visually oriented readers will often read them before the body copy, and *contact information* that tells how to reach you. Your writer should deal with all of these items, including making sure everything is accurate to the best of his or her abilities. Of course, the final proofreading will be up to you.

Copywriting style is not the same as the writing style I'm using here. Copy may use incomplete sentences and a wide range of pacing. It usually has an underlying sales pitch woven into every sentence. When you consider your writer's work, look for *flow*, an organization that carries the theme of the headline naturally through the whole text, an effective *offer* or call to action, and a vibrant, interesting, non–business-speak *tone*. It should be interesting to read, and every word should be there for a reason. Avoid filler and stick to information that is of real benefit to the reader.

Once the copy is in place, the designer takes over. He or she will work up a rough layout for you to look at. I highly recommend you only work with graphic designers who use the latest desktop publishing software—it gives them a great deal of flexibility and saves you money. Your logo becomes a file they can instantly resize and place in any document. They can make changes quickly and run out an instant proof on a laser printer for your approval. The flexibility involved means that when you need a piece put together overnight for an unexpected meeting or event, the designer can incorporate previous work into the new piece while maintaining a consistent, professional message.

If you use a computer at work to create invoices, letters, and other customized business forms, have your designer provide forms and files with your logo that you can print out yourself. If your designer is a market-savvy individual, she'll want to help you maintain a high level of design consistency on all your work because it not only works for you but reflects well on her. Nothing frustrates a designer more than to do a great piece for a client, only to have that great work go out with a homemade-looking letter or other materials.

Printers

Once copy and design are complete and you have approved them in writing, it is time to get printing quotes, prepare final output for the printer, choose paper, and have the job printed. If the piece is an ad, your designer will check with the publication and create a file or output that matches its specifications. This is very important—you send something with the wrong line screen or other technical bloopers, and your ad may come out blurry, discolored, or worse.

Output is simply taking the computer files that are the finished product and turning them into images that the printer can use to make plates for the presses. Often this is done by a service bureau that specializes in this exacting work. Because the technical management of output can be mind-boggling, your designer should handle this step. Output ranges from simple black-and-white laser prints to four-color separations—four perfectly matched pieces of film that must be made into plates and carefully printed by experts. If you are using multiple colors, do not work with a designer who does not have a portfolio showing a lot of color work. This is complex and is what separates experienced designers from those who are just getting started.

I recommend having your designer get printing quotes for you. Not only do designers know the process and who does good work, but they buy printing regularly, making them valued customers of the print shop. You may be able to go to your local quick-print shop and beat their price—but that usually means that the printer is using paper plates that don't hold a tight image over long print runs. They also tend to limit your paper choices and to have problems with quality. These shops are fine for low-budget pieces you'll be using for special events, but you are better off with a skilled pro printer for most long-term pieces.

Once you've got a quote, approved the design and copy, got output, and gone to press, your marketing materials will be in hand soon. All of these production steps are only the prelude to the real challenge: Putting these tools to work for you right now and as long as you're in business. In the next chapter we're going to look at the many print marketing tools available and how to get them out there generating business for you.

CHAPTER 11

PUTTING PRINT MARKETING MATERIALS TO WORK

Before you produce business cards, brochures, or other print marketing tools, you should have a plan for putting them to work. Obviously, this plan should be fully integrated with your personal goals and the strategy in your overall marketing plan. Even without a marketing plan, you really should spend some time figuring out how to get the most out of these tools before you invest time and money in them.

From the perspective of a former ad agency writer, there is nothing more frustrating than creating a great marketing piece, handing it over to a satisfied client, and then running into them a year later and finding out that they never really used it! This happens all the time. The conversation typically goes like this:

"How did that brochure work out for you?"

"Great! Everyone [meaning friends, relatives, and so on] really liked it."

"Are you ready to do another one?"

"No, we still have boxes of them. I really didn't have the time to send them all out—but when we do use them it seems like they work."

Yow! You go through all the work getting these things done and they end up in a closet. Worse, you don't really know if the ones you did use were effective. It's my guess that 75 percent of the marketing materials printed never leave the boxes they arrived in from the printer. The goal of this chapter is to give you enough ideas on how to use those materials that you never have to throw away unused business cards, outdated newsletters, and boxes of glossy four-color brochures that didn't earn their keep.

There are two lessons to keep in mind throughout this chapter and this book. A brochure or business card that never leaves your briefcase is worthless, no matter what it cost you to create. And if you do use these tools, you must develop a system for tracking their effectiveness. This system is the core of modern marketing. It can be as simple as counting responses to a mailing or asking first-time callers where they heard of you. It can be as complex as the arcane but effective testing procedures used by direct response advertising gurus. Either way, the more you know about what worked and what didn't, the more you can fine-tune and target your future marketing, both saving money and making more money. Effective marketers always know how well their marketing is working.

Let's take a look at some typical print marketing tools and some of the ways you can put them to work for you right now, in the real world. We'll start with those common little critters we all take for granted: business cards.

YOUR HIGH-POWER, PORTABLE INFORMATION-CONTACT-MARKETING GIZMOS

Imagine a wallet-size information manager that requires no electricity, can be reproduced in quantity for next to nothing, reminds your customers regularly of your existence, and serves as an instant source of information for reaching you anytime and anywhere. Of course, I'm talking about business cards. My guess is that you already have one, or to be more accurate, several hundred of them. And I'm willing to bet that most of them still reside in that small cardboard box they came in.

There is no mystery to using business cards as a marketing tool. You just have to hand them out as often as possible, preferably several per day. In fact, it's a good idea to set a little goal to get rid of these things as quickly as possible. You may be surprised to know that most people don't automatically toss your card out as soon as you turn away. Instead, cards end up in rotary files, wallets, or planners, or they get entered into a database as soon as the recipient gets back to the office. There are even scanners specifically designed to scan business cards and convert the information they contain into a database of contacts. And *contacts* is the key word here.

Each time you give out a card, you are building on that personal connection you've made with another person. The card is a reminder of that connection. If you practice effective sales techniques, your card will remind people of their interest in what you have to offer. When you hand out a card, always try to get one in exchange. Add this valued contact to your customer list. Because you've actually made personal contact, these names are particularly useful for future sales calls. They are more likely to remember you and respond to your next contact.

So how do you get rid of a thousand business cards (other than tossing them off of a pier)? Here are a few suggestions:

- *Always keep several fresh cards with you.* If your cards get dog-eared, throw them away and use new ones.
- *Always hand out a card at the end of a conversation.* Just say, "Here's a card if you ever need to get hold of me or need help with a project."
- *Attach cards to all outgoing mail.* This includes invoices, bill payments, letters, anything you send.

You never know who is going to open the piece and find your card interesting.

- *Make your card interesting but not gimmicky.* Use high-quality paper, extra colors, a powerful logo, and a tagline that describes your business. Avoid cutesy images, clip art, and puns. The difference in cost between a nicely designed card done on quality paper and the cheap quick-print alternatives is a few dollars—but the way your customers react to them can mean a great deal more. Sometimes having a more professional look can mean getting higher rates for your work or being considered for bigger jobs. Don't cheap out.

- *Make sure you include all of your contact info.* This includes your direct phone number, voice mail number, mailing address, cell phone number, e-mail address, Web URL, fax number, pager number—whatever you've got. The idea is to be instantly accessible. With any luck, we will soon have one number or address for all of these things. If being accessible at home or during odd hours bothers you, you might be in the wrong career; self-employment is not a nine-to-five job. Make yourself available.

- *Consider adding valuable information on the back if it suits your business.* My mortgage broker and realtor both have cards with interest rate amortization tables on the back; I keep their cards handy because of it.

- *Avoid loading your card with too much information.* You want people to call you when they need to know more. The information you do include should list what you offer rather than tell everything you know. It's not a brochure, it's a contact device.
- *Leave cards whenever you get a chance.* All participants at meetings, trade shows, presentations, seminars, and classes you attend ought to leave with one of your cards.
- *Attach cards to all other print materials, including brochures, newsletters, and so on.* This also gives you a place to write a brief personal message on an otherwise impersonal advertising piece. A simple "Give me a call"—or the perennial "Let's do lunch"—may generate another personal contact.
- *Keep your cards up to date.* If you find yourself writing information like e-mail addresses or a clarification of who you are on your cards before you give them out, have them redone with this information on them and throw away the outdated cards.

Business cards are tools. Use them every day. Like every tactic we'll cover, their effectiveness grows as you get more of them out working for you. The card you hand out today may generate business next year. Even if this seems like a long time frame, it won't happen if you don't get that card out now. And remember the power of a little marketing practice every day: Give out three cards a day and you'll have made over a thousand contacts by the end of a year.

BROCHURES: WHAT YOU ARE CAPABLE OF

I've written many brochures for all kinds of businesses. They ranged from one-color photocopied flyers to seven-color, ten-page booklets on heavy varnished stock. Some of those high-end brochures ended up costing several dollars a piece, while the low-budget ones got done for a few cents. Yet I cannot tell you that the $7 brochure is more effective than the 10-cent one. In fact I can think of times when the $7 masterpiece scared away a customer or failed to convey the right message. It all depends on your business and your customers.

In his book *How to Succeed as an Independent Consultant* (Wiley, 1988), Herman Holtz gives a good example of how crazy the world of brochures can be. An expert in working with U.S. government agencies, Holtz says that in order to secure government consulting contracts (the government is the number one employer of consultants), you must have an 8.5 × 11, four-color glossy brochure, no matter what your business is. Government employees file these expensive brochures and pull them out when they get ready to do a request-for-proposal mailing. No fancy brochure, no place in the file. It is just one of the crazy filtering devices used by the government.

These kinds of experiences are what guide your choices in creating and using a brochure. Look at what the industry standard is in your business and do at least as good a job as the best piece you can find. Manufacturer's reps like brochures with perforations that can be inserted into a binder to create a catalog. Some brochures end up in literature racks with spaces only for three- or four-fold pieces that fit in a #10 envelope. Mailing requirements may determine design. An expensive brochure in a competitive low-budget business like home repairs may scare off potential customers, yet a high-end kitchen designer may need to fill her brochure with eye-catching photos of dream kitchens.

Besides the level of gloss, you must consider the message. Brochures may cover a specific product or service or act as a catalog of the many options you offer. The most typical format and the one you'll probably use as a self-employed person is the capabilities brochure. A capabilities brochure combines a description of what you offer or are capable of with a sales pitch designed to get the reader to avail themselves of those valuable capabilities. It is a universal marketing tool that expands on your personal contacts and initial contact pieces like business cards.

Brochures are rarely successful for first contacts. They are follow-up and reinforcement information.

One of the most common mistakes a small business owner makes is attempting to use brochures as a substitute for personal contact and selling. A typical scenario involves a cold call made to a potential new customer. After the self-employed business caller gives a name and a brief explanation of the call, the listener interrupts and asks for some written information. The caller takes the address and hangs up, feeling that they have made a good contact—after all, it wasn't like the ones who just cut the connection.

What has actually happened is that they have been brushed off. The brochure has become a tool for the customer to get rid of the caller. While I'll be covering telephone sales in Chapter 14, I'll let you know now that this is the result of an unplanned phone call. The goal of any prospecting call, networking event, or other initial contact is always the same: To get an appointment to make a sales presentation. You're better off brushing aside the "send out a brochure" response and sticking to setting up a specific time to meet. Then you can give them the brochure.

So what do you do with brochures? You use them to follow up, to flesh out a brief meeting, to add color and visual impact to a sales call, and to respond to unsolicited requests for information. Here is a checklist of some of the ways to put your brochures to work:

- *Send them as follow-ups.* They should go out along with a personal letter in response to any request for information and any meeting or casual networking contact. In this case, they are a way for both you and your new contact to qualify your interest in each other. (See Chapter 14 for more on *qualifying* a prospect—that is, finding out basic info about the possibility of doing business—and Chapter 17 for a detailed discussion of qualification and sales.)

- *Send them to everyone on your mailing lists.* (More about lists in Chapter 12!) And not just once—they should go out once every six months to remind people of your existence. Always include a brief letter or note.

- *Leave them in places where potential customers may pick them up.* This includes stores, convention centers, worksite eating areas, literature racks, and so on. You may need to get permission to leave them in some places. Don't leave them any old place; put them in places where qualified prospects will see them. Be creative. I recently attended a local museum's showing of a classic film. A New York City film school had a rack full of brochures for their crash course in film-making. Many of the film buffs attending the screening were picking them up. A company I work with that provides home care services for seniors leaves their brochures in pharmacies and hospitals, both logical places. However, their best response has come from airports! It turns out that many traveling executives are concerned about having reliable care for their aging parents, particularly when they are out of town.

- *Always use brochures at the end of sales presentations rather than the beginning.* A brochure is a great reminder if the recipient reads it later; it is a distraction if they read it when you're face to face.
- *Ask your satisfied customers if you can leave a few brochures with them for referrals.* This only works if the customer is a referral kind of person. These are people who thrive on making connections between resources they know.

Brochures are tools. Get them out working for you now. I've had clients who were hesitant to hand out brochures, saying things like "They cost me six bucks a piece!" This is ridiculous—but it happens more often than you'd think. If you hand out a hundred brochures a month and get even one new customer, they have probably justified their existence. However, when combined with a concerted effort driven by a marketing plan, these tools should generate a much higher response.

SALES LETTERS

One of the least expensive and most effective print marketing tools is the simple sales letter. With the advent of computers and high-quality printers that use regular letterhead paper, you can take a generic letter, tailor it to an individual customer, and print it in moments. If it is well written (a job for copy pros) it will help generate responses and appointments while reinforcing your customers' confidence level in your relationship.

A sales letter is a brief letter designed to get a response. That's all. It is a prospecting tool created to get prospects to respond to your marketing and to give you the opportunity to turn those prospects into customers. It can take the form of a get-acquainted letter, an update on new business developments, a keeping-in-touch letter, a personal press release extolling an accomplishment or recognition you've received, a let's-do-lunch note, or any other message that says "let's talk."

Sales letters must always be included with any mailings of brochures or announcements. The letter builds the personal aspect of your relationship with the customer in a way that a preprinted brochure cannot. It allows you to customize your message and stress points relevant to that particular customer or group of customers. You can use several different sales letters to target several different types of customers with the same offer. You can also tell them about specials, late-breaking news, or info they can use.

One advantage of running a one-person business is that you can customize your marketing in a personal way because your targeted markets may be very small. Almost any word processing program or contact management program can customize your letters to any database or mailing list and spew out letter after letter, each bearing a personal address and greeting. Add your signature and they become real letters, indistinguishable from personal notes written for each person. In these days of an endless barrage of marketing offers, the more personal you can make your message, the better.

When I was writing freelance ad copy full time, I worked from a list of about 50 ad agency contacts that I assembled myself from various sources. I kept this list up to date and accurate and regularly sent letters out telling about the recent work I'd done and letting them know about my specialties. Because my list was small, I'd customize each letter quickly, importing names and addresses from a database file and then adding personal notes where applicable. These went out four or five times a year along with a business card. They generated enough business to keep me busy without doing any other marketing! Of course, I did follow up with other mailings and regularly attended meetings of the local advertising community so that people would have a face to put with the message.

Unless you're a skilled ad writer, I recommend having a pro write these letters. They will put a spin on your message, organize it in a concise and readable fashion, and keep the selling message consistent. Take their version, put it on your letterhead, and use it. Eventually, you may adapt it or start to learn how to write effective sales letters yourself. You can also get books of generic sales letters that you can customize to fit your business.

Try to resist the temptation to tell too much in your letter. If you really want to send a lot of useful information out, use our next print marketing tool, the newsletter.

Newsletters

We've all seen dozens of newsletters ranging in style and substance from homegrown missives created on a computer to glossy corporate inserts thrown in with everything from bank statements to phone bills. What most newsletters have in common is a format that is brief, direct, devoid of traditional advertising, and eminently practical. They are, in fact, letters with news and carry that personal letter feel.

Newsletters are often viewed as being more valuable than their size might warrant because they contain relevant, concise, and profitable information. Many investment and industry-specific subscription newsletters are very expensive, sometimes as high as $250 to $1,000 per year. Their subscribers pay the price because the information is worth it to them. With the advent of the Internet and the World Wide Web, these newsletters are undergoing a change in format and delivery method. Newsletters used for marketing purposes are also experiencing these changes as many companies large and small seek to generate interest in their Web sites. However, there is a fundamental difference between newsletters sent by mail (postal or e-mail) and those sites on the Web: Mailed newsletters require no effort by the customer, they simply appear, ready to be read or discarded as the reader chooses. Creating a marketing tool that requires active participation by the customer (like a Web site) is a much more difficult task. For these reasons, I still believe that newsletters and other print (or e-mail) tools will remain valuable.

So how can a small business profit with newsletters? By filling them with useful, current, interesting material that is relevant to your customers. The newsletter can be nothing more than a letter, written by you, updating the readers on new developments you've come across and information you feel is valuable to them, along with a mild sales pitch. The purpose of newsletters as marketing tools is to add value to the customer's relationship with you rather than to serve as a brochure or other type of sales tool.

Newsletters do not have to be fancy, four-color, twelve-page pieces laden with graphics. In fact, they often work better as homegrown, succinct, and interesting underground-style documents. Assembled on your computer, printed at a local copy shop, and mailed several times per year, these simple pieces can generate a lot of goodwill and profitable business.

Newsletters are effective for any business with a steady customer list as opposed to those who sell a service or product once and lose track of the buyer. Retail stores, service businesses, and freelancers can use newsletters in lieu of more complex (and expensive) marketing tools. You can send them on their own or follow the example of bigger companies and piggyback them with other mailings, including invoices, sales letters, brochures, and so on. I think it's better to send them off alone because it adds one more contact to your overall plan, gradually resulting in a more solid business relationship.

What do you put in your newsletter? Make a brief list of regular features and work from it each time you put the letter together. Look at classic newsletters like the *Kiplinger Letter*, which has a single paragraph on each news item. This can be done on one two-sided page and still be effective. Include info on new products and developments, personal stories from recent experiences that illustrate a point, tips on maximizing the usefulness of whatever products you sell, and other relevant info. For example, a natural foods store owner might put together a newsletter on new products and ways to use existing ones. When sent to a mailing list compiled in the store, it serves as a regular contact and reminder to steady customers. A kitchen designer might feature articles about new appliances, a Q&A column, or examples of unique problems she faced and the solutions she developed.

A graphic design agency might use a newsletter to show the fun, creative side of its work, giving its clients a look at the wilder possibilities of the medium. As a marketing writer and consultant, I would do a newsletter featuring tips on building a business with tactics like those in this book. Even a plumber or contractor can add value by sending off a quarterly letter telling how to get a building permit or resolve a contract dispute.

Newsletters are effective because they do not look or read like marketing pieces. Instead they offer useful, real-world information, building value with your customers. Keep the newsletter simple and concise and you'll find your customers thanking you for sending it out. This leads to one of the most effective tactics you can use to build a one-person business: information-of-interest mail.

INFORMATION OF INTEREST

Imagine one day I'm reading and I come across an article I know will be of interest to several of my clients. Perhaps it deals with another business's success story or a problem-solving technique. I do a quick summary of the article, mentioning where it's from, and send it off to my customers with a brief note saying I thought of them when I saw it. This is what I call information-of-interest mail, and it is a very powerful tactic for self-employed people. It requires little time and serves the same purpose as sending out gifts or referrals because it is a valued effort made solely in the interest of the

recipient. The value comes because you made an unsolicited effort based on consideration and interest in the
reader's life and business.

Information of interest need not be restricted to articles. I've had great success sending out half a dozen
copies of a book that I thought would resonate with the
interests of my customers. The cost may have been a
hundred dollars but the results were worth it. For
example, in my reading I came across a book called
The Artist's Way by Julia Cameron and Mark Bryan
(Tarcher/Putnam, 1992). The book dealt with artists'
blocks and ways to enhance creativity. I found it impressive and immediately thought of several people who
would really enjoy it, including clients of both of my
businesses. The musicians who use my recording studio,
the creative directors I work with at advertising agencies, and the business owners who use me as a consultant all have an interest in the creative process. I've sent
out several dozen copies of this book alone over the past
few years—and each time, the response has been great.
In one case, I spent over an hour on the phone with the
CEO of a fast-growing company, discussing the book
and the challenge of remaining creative in a corporate
environment. That contact has resulted in profitable and
interesting work, valuable referrals, and a friendship.

Information of interest need be nothing more than
a clipping and a sticky note. Staple your card to the
clipping and you'll get calls. Follow up with a brochure

and sales letter and you'll get business based on mutual interests, the best kind.

Postcards

Postcards are my favorite low-cost, highly effective print marketing tools. They are cheap to produce, cheap to mail, and people almost always read them before they toss them. If they contain a compelling message or image, they may get stuck on a bulletin board, serving as a constant reminder of your business. There are several ways to effectively deploy these little marketing weapons.

Do a series of cards rather than one. If they have a message, have the series build on the message step by step in a clever way. Your writer and graphic designer can make the series work together visually and intellectually. You can have the whole series printed at once, saving considerable money. Send one out every month, and your customers will be forced to recognize it.

Have fun with cards. They are throwaways, so don't hesitate to be a little irreverent or have a good-natured laugh at yourself. If you're a visual artist, postcards are a way to gradually expose your market to carefully chosen portfolio pieces, month after month. The prices of color postcards are very low if you deal with national specialist printers who do nothing but cards. You can find their ads in fine arts and crafts magazines.

Keep the message brief and use the image side of the card to tell the story. Use cards to announce events you're involved with or new products and services. Use cards to test new lists or expand the range of your mailings. If you normally mail 100 pieces, consider sending 500 cards once every six months to test the waters on a bigger scale. Add any responses you get to your regular list.

SIGNS

A lot of you work out of your homes and probably never consider the use of signs as a marketing tool—and the local zoning board might object if you tried to post anything. Others who run walk-in businesses know that signs can and do generate business. But you don't have to have a store or visible business location to make use of signage.

Signage covers everything from the gold letters on the entrance of a law firm to a huge billboard on a freeway seen by thousands every day. They appear on vehicles, lawns, at trade shows and seminars, and in airports and public transport. They can merely tell someone they've found you or shout out a visual message to a harried commuter. They're made of everything from cardboard to laser-cut wood and vinyl to neon-filled tubing glowing in the night. They work because we look for them and are used to seeing them. They are also one of the oldest marketing devices on the planet.

Originally, they always featured an image along with words (or even without words) so that illiterate customers would see an anvil and know they'd found a blacksmith or a wheel for a wheelwright. These visual images were the first logotypes.

Even if you provide information services out of a home office and seldom meet your customers face to face, there may be a place for signs in your marketing plan. A discreet vehicle sign may generate calls. Your presentations at shows and seminars require signage. You're far better off getting a compelling sign rather than relying on the generic block-letter sign supplied by the show sponsor.

Signage is another area to enlist your graphic designer rather than using the design services of the sign maker. Use your logo, typeface, name, and tagline, if applicable. If you have a store or retail location, lighting the sign is almost as important as having one. Place signs so they can be read from passing cars—and make them legible. When I was a young rock musician, we used posters to promote gigs. Our only rule in creating a poster was that it be readable from a moving car!

Sign companies can usually make any kind of sign you want. Use them as consultants to help you choose what you need. There is a bewildering variety of materials, options, and price ranges. If you use a car sign, you can get a removable one that turns your car from a business vehicle to a private one in moments. If your business is located in a particularly busy area, you can use neon to cut through the visual clutter. Whatever you use, remember that signs are a constant reminder of your existence and can generate a lot of customer contacts over a short period. Eventually those contacts will result in business.

OTHER PRINT MARKETING STUFF

Conventional paper printed materials are not the only print marketing items out there. You can have your logo printed on everything from baseballs to cheesecakes. Consider the following when planning your marketing:

- Bumper stickers
- Coffee mugs
- Gift items like desk accessories and other ad specialties
- Refrigerator magnets
- Pens
- T-shirts, hats, and other casual apparel

These ad specialty items are available in a mind-boggling range of colors, materials, and styles. If you use them as gifts, get high quality; if they are giveaways, you can buy the less expensive ones. Things like coffee mugs, T-shirts, and hats are moving billboards for your business that get seen day in and day out. Make sure they have a phone number on them.

People love free stuff. Anyone who has attended a trade show knows that even high-power executives will fight over freebies and leave with bags overflowing with junk. You can use this compulsion to generate a lot of traffic at your booth. One photo dealer I know gives away a 35mm camera every hour at the big trade shows he attends. The only catch is that you must be there to win. The result? Every hour he has a mob of people around his booth, many coming by every hour on the hour, giving him ample opportunities to pitch his products and get to know potential customers. For the price of 15 or 20 inexpensive cameras he gets at cost, he has nonstop traffic while his competitors twiddle their thumbs.

Marketing materials that attract your customers are powerful tools. They create excitement and interest, they constantly remind people of your existence, and they offer instant reference when someone needs to reach you. To take full advantage of their potential, they must be well executed and you must get them out of your office and into the hands of your customers. Your marketing plan should include plenty of opportunities to do so.

CHAPTER 12

THE DIRECT ROUTE: DIRECT RESPONSE MARKETING TECHNIQUES

This chapter covers the self-employed person's most powerful prospecting tactic: *direct response marketing*. A prospecting tactic is any marketing tool that reaches out to prospective customers and gives you the opportunity to turn them into paying, current customers. Prospecting is anything you do to make an effective first contact that eventually gives you the opportunity to sell that prospect on the value of doing business with you.

You could prospect the old-fashioned way by going out and knocking on doors at random until you found a likely prospect. Of course, this would take a lot of time and would be incredibly inefficient, not to mention exhausting. But what if there was a way to only knock on those doors whose owners both needed your services and had the ability to pay for them? Knocking on doors would suddenly become a lot more profitable. Direct response marketing puts you outside the best doorways in town for your particular business and prequalifies each and every prospect so that you know their interests and needs before you ring the bell.

Direct response marketing is any marketing tactic that targets a specific audience, delivers a message, and provides an immediate way to respond to that message. The response is measurable and therefore predictable—after you've tested your tactics. These attributes (targeting, direct delivery, response mechanism, testing, and measurability) are what set direct response apart from normal advertising techniques. Done methodically and creatively, direct response delivers the most effective and profitable return on your marketing investment. Done haphazardly, it is the equivalent of flushing money down the drain.

The most common example of direct response is direct mail—you get a packet of paper that tells you about an offer and provides you with an incredibly effortless way to respond via prepaid business reply mail or a toll-free phone number. Other direct response tactics include telemarketing by phone, TV, and radio ads that feature a toll-free number and credit card payment, including those relentless half-hour advertisements known as infomercials, coupon ads in print media, print ads featuring toll-free numbers, and any other advertising that is aimed directly at a motivated list of customers.

We are also starting to see direct response e-mail and other electronic tactics. Web sites that users must navigate to are not direct response because they do not go to a passive target audience, though they often have other direct response attributes like measurability and a response mechanism.

Confused? Let's go back to those direct mail pieces we all receive every day and look at how a small business like yours might effectively use them. Before you even consider a mailing, you have to know what kind of people you are going to mail to. You could mail to a random selection of addresses, but that would be unprofitable because you have no way of knowing if any of your mail is getting to anyone who might need your services. So the first step is to target a group that will be interested in your message.

Large companies mail pieces out in the millions because they have the ability to respond to thousands of replies while enjoying a significant cost advantage through economies of scale. A tiny company like your own enjoys a very different advantage: Your needs are so small that you can focus in on a very specific list of prospects and tailor your marketing in a very personal and powerful way to their needs. The first step is to create or find a list or lists to begin with.

YOUR MAILING LIST

Every business should have an accurate and up-to-date customer list divided into three categories: present customers, past customers, and prospective customers. Without such a list, you are letting all your marketing efforts drain through your fingers because you reinvent the wheel each time you go out to find customers. These three categories are in order of importance. Present customers are the most valuable because they know of you already and have proved they have a current need for your products. Take care of them first and make sure that they always receive all your marketing, preferably in advance of other groups. Past customers are a close second because they know you and your services and may have simply slipped away or been snatched up by a competitor. One of the biggest mistakes self-employed people make is losing touch with past customers. They often represent an untapped vein of additional business and referrals.

The third category, prospective customers, is the broadest and the least reliable. However, because the world is so large and supports so many special interests, prospective customers represent an alluring potential for growth and the opportunity to increase profits and find more interesting work. Much of the targeting used in direct response is designed to help you choose the best groups to market to from this world of potential.

Remember that advantage I mentioned of being small? It includes the fact that many self-employed people need do no more than assemble a list of current and past customers and market only to them. You add new names as you get referrals while you stay focused on a proven list. In Chapter 11, I told how I used a list of ad agency creative directors to sell my copywriting skills. That list had 47 names on it, a minuscule number when compared to the mega lists you can rent or compile in almost any area. However, my mailings to that short list generated enough work that I found myself raising rates and turning down the more marginal or uninteresting projects it created.

It is not unusual for a self-employed person to have a list with one name on it. This often occurs when someone leaves a corporate job with the promise that his or her former employer will send work if they set up on their own. As many of these newly minted self-employees find out, this is a recipe for disaster—illustrating the proverb about "putting all your eggs in one basket." If you've done this, read on and diversify your mix even if it means taking on less profitable projects from other sources. Even one other list member divides your risk by up to 50 percent.

By the way, one of the most effective strategies you can use if you deal with a large company is to go after business from other sources in that company. Because marketing is always done person to person, you're probably dealing with a limited number of individuals in a single department. You can leverage your track record at that company by marketing to other people in similar but noncompeting areas of the same company, using your current contact as a referral. This effectively doubles your current customer list. Going further, you can look for similar companies that are not in direct competition with your current customer and use your experience to get you in the door. Often, the executives of these neighboring companies know each other, and sometimes dropping a name will lend you the cachet you need to generate interest. In both of these cases, your direct response campaign may only consist of a few letters or lunches.

If you are starting out cold with no customers, you can compile a list of prospects by joining associations that provide member directories, going through reference works in the library (my ad agency list was originally compiled from the *Advertising Red Book,* an industry bible), or dealing with list brokers. List brokers usually rent lists at a rate per thousand names for one-time use. The lists arrive on mailing labels, computer disks, or special Cheshire labels for mailing machines. (Warning: brokers are serious about one-time use, and salt their lists with names that let them know if you try to use the list more than once.) Rental lists cover almost any group imaginable and range from $50 to $1,000 per thousand names, depending on the value of the list. Generally, the names on cheap lists come from directories and phone books; expensive lists include very specific, up-to-date sets of names with a high response rate for certain kinds of offers. You can find list brokers in the Yellow Pages under Mailing Lists. Call a few of the national companies and ask for catalogs. They are an enlightening read for the neophyte direct marketer.

Managing Your List

It's important to set up some kind of management system for your list that helps you keep it up to date and accurate. People move, retire, change jobs, and change positions constantly in today's society. Because personal, one-to-one marketing is so important to self-employed people, it is vital that you are accurate when you contact anyone and that you always have a specific name to send your marketing materials to. Mail addressed to Owner or Partner is inevitably headed for the circular file.

Fortunately, computers make list management very easy. A whole category of software products, known as contact management software, competes for the chance to make these tasks very easy for you. You can use these programs to build a customer list and customize it easily without any programming savvy. Most will print standard labels on any printer, generate customized sales letters on your letterhead, and help you track contacts. They usually have a companion planner program that helps you create a marketing calendar. They are inexpensive and constitute a real break-through for very small businesses, giving us the same tools previously enjoyed by our larger competitors.

In my studio business, I routinely enter every new contact I make as I collect business cards, names, ad-dresses, phone and fax numbers, e-mail addresses, and other contact info. Spending a few minutes per week making calls to fill in incomplete information will not only keep your list accurate, it will also keep you aware of personnel changes that may affect your business. Just call the receptionist and say you're verifying some in-formation. She will usually be glad to help.

If you don't have a computer, plan on getting one. Even an inexpensive model will easily handle every-thing most businesses require. Until you get a computer, you can run a small list by purchasing sheets of mailing labels from your copy shop. Get the same ones they can run through their copiers and write or type your names on them. Save your originals as master copies and have photocopies made when you need to do a mailing. This process is inefficient and unwieldy when your list grows—but it will get you started.

CD-ROMs now offer the computer user many of the benefits of rented lists without the expense, al-though they are somewhat less accurate and timely. I have a CD-ROM of the Business Yellow Pages for the whole United States. I can search through it by name, location, business type, and state and I can print labels with it or export the information into any database. It features a search engine that uses *SIC codes,* a standard list of business types created by the federal government. It's amazingly fast and I can generate a list almost instantly to fit any category.

Lists don't have to consist of individual names and mailing addresses. There are e-mail lists, Web site lists, association lists, and numerous other lists. Lists of subscribers to various magazines are popular. Running a local cooking school? Try using a list of *Bon Appétit* subscribers in the ZIP codes around your area. Offering your moving services? Try a list of local real estate agents. The possibilities are endless.

THE GLOBAL-LOCAL QUESTION

One common mistake self-employed people make is to limit their marketing to their own geographic area. Instead of thinking of your market as your town, think of it as a global community that seeks specialized knowledge that you can sell anywhere. Direct marketing can make this easier. For instance, most HVAC (heating, ventilation, and air conditioning) installers work in a limited area. One that I know began specializing in building HVAC systems for clean rooms used in the semiconductor industry. Soon he had the local market covered and realized that he could expand his operations nationally. Now he and two employees fly around the country consulting on these specialized installations.

He no longer does the work but instead trains local contractors to do it and charges top dollar. He started with a direct mailing to 40 HVAC contracting companies nationwide and he has never looked back.

AN OFFER AND A CALL TO ACTION

Lists and targeting go hand in hand. So does the next aspect, the offer. Whatever medium you choose to reach your customers, it must contain a compelling offer. Writing effective direct response is closer to a science than any other kind of copywriting. Direct response writers have an arcane list of tactics and gimmicks they use in every offering. Each of these devices has a recognized and measurable effect on the recipient. Ever wonder why every subscription solicitation you get in the mail has a free issue offer, a sticker you place on an order form and a folded paper with the words "If you've decided not to order . . ." (or something similar) on the outside? Each of these devices adds to the response rate. Sales letters have devices like bold print, comments that appear handwritten, color used in certain places, and so on. The length and message are carefully constructed and the actual call to action appears several times throughout the package.

All of these devices, gimmicks, and paraphernalia have a specific intent: To convey an offer and involve the reader in the process of acting on that offer. The offer must be presented in terms of the benefits that the reader will reap. Certain power words are important—including that classic, *FREE!* Free offers, free estimates, free consultations, free-when-purchased-with, and other freebies generate response. Whatever buzz words, gimmicks, and tricks you use, they should always offer a concrete benefit to the recipient.

To learn more about the whole process of direct mail and other direct response copywriting, check out any of the excellent books directed at mail order business owners—they can make fascinating reading. (I've listed some in the Resources section.) Direct response copywriting can be a crazy profession and many of its practitioners are full of hilarious stories of successes and failures. What makes them stand out as consummate marketers is their intense desire to learn from these successes and failures so that the next offer is stronger, pulling even better. Their interest in results stems from another important aspect of direct response marketing: *measurability.*

HOW WELL DID IT DO?

That question, when applied to many marketing tactics, is a tough one to answer. We often don't see immediate results from conventional advertising, networking, publicity, and other marketing tools because those results are spread out over time and space. They get results—but the results are not immediate and measurable. With direct response, they are immediate and measurable because direct response asks the recipient to respond in a very specific way. For instance, if you send a mailing with a reply card and an 800 telephone number, you'll know very quickly just how effective that offer was. You can literally count the responses, compare the total to the exact size of the mailing, and generate a response figure as a percentage. That percentage is a reliable indicator of how additional mailings of that specific offer will perform to that specific list.

This measurability means that you can tinker with every aspect of your direct response campaign until you find the most effective combination and then increase your mailings or ads to increase your sales. This is because you can test small mailings and fine-tune until you know what works. For the self-employed person, this testing may simply consist of trying various tactics on your small lists and then going with the ones that work. First you must build in ways to measure the response.

We've all seen codes on mailing labels. Those codes tell direct mail gurus what lists your name came from, when the mailing went out, and what mailing it was. When a business reply card goes back to an advertiser, they make a record of that information and use it to measure the effectiveness of the lists they rent and other techniques they use. So how does a one-person business do the same?

First, you always ask every new customer or inquirer where they heard of you. If you use a rental list for a mailing, code your address or phone number with a department number or name that tells you what list the caller was on. Keep it simple—but keep track. The successful lists and tactics are the ones to spend the majority of your marketing dollars and time on.

THIS IS JUST A TEST

Huge direct marketing companies test constantly. They test pricing, packaging, offers, wording, various elements like envelope copy, color, and size, typestyles, and every imaginable aspect of their promotions. Because they mail in huge quantities, they don't want to waste money on ineffective offers and they test on parts of various lists, usually using a selection of names from a list. If the list has 100,000 names, they may pick every tenth name and do a smaller mailing. If it works, then they mail to the whole list.

For a small business, this kind of testing isn't practical. However, because your list is small, you'll have your own instant response to every solicitation and you'll soon know what works best for you. Focus on the successes and don't spend time and energy trying to make something work that doesn't generate profitable responses. This is true of every aspect of your marketing. When something does not work as planned, go on to the next tactic or rework that one. And don't spend a lot of energy trying to do business with someone who's not interested. Just drop the name and go on to the next. It's much more efficient to focus on what works and on motivated customers than to spend your time and money trying to convince someone to do business with you.

BEYOND THE MAILS

Although I've focused on direct mail in this chapter, there are many other forms of direct response. In fact, you can insert a response mechanism into almost any marketing tactic. Ads should include 800 toll-free numbers if they reach out of your local calling area. These numbers are very inexpensive and can ring on your normal phone. The phone company charges you by the minute; there may be a token monthly fee as well; but if you negotiate, it is often possible to eliminate or reduce such fees. And if it bothers you to pay for incoming calls, remember, the person who makes this call is a highly motivated prospect who is ready to buy.

You can include response cards in seminar and trade show materials, have sales letters inserted in magazines and newsletters, and use the phone to reach out to potential customers (for telephone selling, see Chapter 14). However you choose to reach out, remember that the direct route is the most effective route to new customers and a vital tactic for keeping your current customers interested.

ABOUT EXTENDING CREDIT

The ability to extend instant credit is one of the reasons for the explosion of direct response advertising. If you can take major credit cards, you will get more sales—the customer has the funds instantly available, can pay back over time, and can give in to impulses as a result. If you have a product line you sell direct to end users (as opposed to distributors or middlemen), then you should arrange to become a merchant card vendor with the major credit card companies. Even though they charge various fees, the increase in potential business for you and convenience for your customers can make it well worth while.

Unfortunately, getting the ability to take credit cards is very difficult for home-based businesses. Banks are wary of any business without a concrete, business-only location because of the many scams and frauds perpetrated on their customers by fly-by-night businesses. In fact, they will send a photographer out to photograph your business location to prove it exists before they approve your application! If you work at home, you're going to have problems. Eventually, this may change—but for now you have to be creative to get merchant status if you work at home.

There are many companies offering services that help you get such status. Be forewarned that many are rip-offs, charging exorbitant up-front fees, high monthly terminal rents, and high percentage of purchase fees. Do your research and try other sources before going this route.

Start with your local commercial banks. If you have a good, creditworthy business relationship with a bank, you may be able to leverage it into an account, particularly if the bank clears its own credit card transactions. If they only act as a broker for another bank, you'll be less likely to get in. If they turn you down, try another bank and keep going until you get somewhere. Some of my clients have had luck getting merchant status by using a cash management account or CMA from a major stock and bond brokerage firm. These accounts are checking accounts that allow you to sweep unused money into investments when you don't need it. I've found them more flexible about granting merchant status than many banks, in part because they require a minimum balance of up to ten thousand dollars (not as big a figure as it sounds if you have your investment or retirement funds there.)

Once you get merchant status, you have the ability to extend credit with limited risk to you. You get paid immediately and don't have to chase delinquent accounts. You'll pay a monthly fee for transaction approval and 1.5 percent to 4 percent of sales. If it makes a significant improvement in cash flow, then it can pay for itself. Accepting credit also is a customer service that may get you business that your competitors miss out on.

Looking Ahead

The future of marketing is direct response. Full Internet access in every home and other online services will mean that any business, large or small, will have equal access to every consumer in the world as they get connected. Conventional distribution systems that favor large companies will fall by the wayside as the information economy makes it possible for the little guy to sell anywhere to anyone direct. By starting in now with even a simple direct mail campaign, you're preparing your business for marketing in the next century.

CHAPTER 13

ADVERTISING:
THE CONTACT SPORT

To some readers, it may seem strange that there has been little mention of advertising up till now in *Marketing for the Self-Employed*. That's because advertising is only one aspect of marketing and because advertising is a double-edged sword for the very small business. It can be very effective when done well. However, it can also be expensive and can cause unforeseen problems—including attracting too much or the wrong kind of work. Like all the tactics in this section, it works best in the context of an overall plan, as one powerful tool among many.

The classic small business advertising scenario runs something like this: The advertising salesperson for a local media outlet like a radio station or newspaper approaches the business owner, offering a special deal on a few ads, which the outlet will produce as part of the package. The owner mulls it over and decides to give it a shot. The ads run, time goes by, and the business owner doesn't gain enough business to cover the advertising expense. The next time someone comes up and tries to sell advertising, the owner says, "We tried it, but it doesn't work for businesses like ours and it costs us a fortune."

I've seen this situation many times while working with an ad agency specializing in small business marketing. It is full of classic errors and misconceptions about how advertising works. Advertising, like most of the tactics in this book, is a contact sport. We all face a barrage of ads, as many as 1500 daily by many estimates. As a result, we tune out all the advertising that doesn't immediately address some problem we're dealing with. Even the most compelling or entertaining advertising won't cause us to go out and buy unless we have some underlying momentum to do so. This underlying momentum often develops out of an ongoing series of contacts between us and an advertiser who is selling a service or product we may need. It takes time and repetition for any ad to break through the barrage and attract our motivated attention.

Failure to run an ad long enough and consistently enough is the first mistake most small businesses make when buying media time. Marketing Guru Jay Conrad Levinson estimates that the average consumer must see an ad 27 times before being ready and willing to patronize the business! He describes a process of gradual recognition combined with a building of trust based on seeing a consistent message over time. In my experience, he is right. So my first guideline for advertising is:

- *It's better to run a small, simple ad every week forever than a big, flashy ad two or three times.* For proof, consider the small ad sections at the back of most national magazines. There are ads running that I have been reading all my life. They are basically unchanged from the original concept. These ads work and have continued to work for many years.

The second mistake commonly made is to let a media salesperson (or account executive as the euphemism goes) choose where and when you advertise. For instance, the offer may involve a set of radio spots at what appears to be a great price, especially when they throw the ad production in for (allegedly) free. The price and quantity make it alluring. Often these spots are in bad time slots or on stations or publications that don't suit your business because your target audience isn't there. The second guideline for advertising is:

- *Choose your media based on your customers' habits.* If you know your target group of customers, then you should have a pretty good idea of what they read, what they listen to, and what they watch. A highly targeted media choice is worth paying extra money for. Look at trade magazines, specialized newsletters, association publications, advertising around radio and TV shows that feature a topic relevant to your business, and so on. If you start advertising regularly, consider using a media buying consultant to negotiate rates, time slots, and page locations, and to find new media that fit your business.

The next mistake lies in the content of the ads themselves. Producing great advertising is an art—and the overworked and harried staff producers and graphic designers at the media office seldom have the time or talent to practice it. Do you want that ad salesperson (whoops, account executive) writing your ad in the car on the way to his next appointment? How about having the same DJ voice talent doing your ad who does 50 percent of the other ads on the same station? Do they know your business? Rule #3 is:

- *Have your advertising produced by the same creative team that does your brochures and other marketing.* Not only will you have a consistent message that reinforces itself each time your customers see or hear it, you'll have handsome ads that sell instead of amateurish, local-sounding ad bites. Look at ads that grab you and find out why.

SHOULD YOU ADVERTISE?

Sometimes the errors are compounded by the question of whether a business should advertise at all. Some businesses will rely on advertising for 90 percent of their business. Others, like freelance writers or consultants, may need no advertising—or at most, a regular ad in a carefully chosen trade magazine or newsletter. You should advertise if:

- *You need to reach large numbers of prospects.* Retail stores, businesses that sell a single product without repeat sales, and businesses without loyal customers have a constant need for more customers. Advertising can reach mass markets.

- *You are in a very competitive business and your competition advertises successfully.* Piggybacking your ad campaign onto a competitor's is a proven technique because you offer an alternative for comparison shopping and you take advantage of all the recognition developed by the competition's ad presence. Imitating success works.

- *Advertising is the primary way prospects expect to find your business sector.* Plumbers always run Yellow Pages ads because that is where everyone turns when they need a plumber. Almost no one uses the Yellow Pages to find writers or furniture makers. Generally, you know you need to advertise if all of your competition runs large, consistent ads in the same media.

■ *Advertising can reinforce your networking, word of mouth and referral business by giving you an improved recognition factor.* It enhances your credibility when someone sees your ads and then hears of you from another source.

Many self-employed people do not need to advertise. Very specialized skills and services directed toward specialized businesses usually don't need ads—the word-of-mouth network does the job. Businesses with easily targeted customers are better off using direct response marketing that can be personalized in a way advertising cannot. The basic rule is to look at your successful competition and see if they advertise regularly. The two keys words here are *successful* and *regularly.* Many businesses run one-time-only ads for events or in special publications like annual directories or for seminars or other one-time needs. Regular advertising, month after month, indicates that something is working for them that you should look into.

Another primary reason not to advertise is your ability to handle volume. Even a small trade magazine may reach thousands of highly targeted prospects and the response may be more than you can handle. This can generate ill will when you cannot deliver on your promise as advertised. Start small and ramp up as the response builds—and stop before you drown in success.

One of the most common reasons for not advertising is the expense involved. Taking the plunge and spending lavishly on untested ads can be dangerous. However, the opposite can also be true: Not advertising because of money may mean leaving a lot of valuable business to others.

MONEY AND ADVERTISING

Advertising is expensive, especially if you have not done it before and don't know if it will work for you. Like every marketing outlay, it is an investment in the future of your business and results often come in the future as the ads build recognition. There are considerable up-front costs for design, writing, films, tapes, studio rental, and other production steps. Fortunately, the results of these production investments can and should last for a long time. There is no benefit in changing the style and substance of your ads on a regular basis. Gradual changes to introduce new products or target new markets can use existing design and adapt existing copy. Once you've paid the start-up costs, the ad materials become a useful asset.

The easiest way to pay for ads is to start out simple and small, test the waters, and use what you've learned to plan any upgrades. Track responses by always asking new customers where they heard of you; put any additional money into those areas that get responses. If you feel you need a Yellow Pages or other directory ad, look at the competition and pick a size similar to a close competitor who has been around for a while. These ads really benefit from professional design and copy because most directory advertisers use the media's staff to create their ads. Make yours stand out even if it is smaller (and cheaper) by having it done by pros.

When you decide to advertise, add the cost of the ads to your monthly overhead and run them for six months or more. You must commit to this strategy to reap the real benefits of advertising. By tracking results, spending a regular amount, and running frequent, consistent ads, you'll eventually see your money multiplied in the form of new business.

CLASSIFIED ADS

If you have an extremely small marketing budget and want to try advertising, consider classified ads. Inexpensive to produce and buy, these ads are the mainstay of many self-employed people. Many small businesses prosper using classified ads that run every week or month in media catering to their customers. If you run them, buy several months in advance to take advantage of frequency discounts. But remember, the lead time for many print media can be months in advance—start planning your ad buys now.

THE INTERNET AND ADVERTISING

Almost every business these days is considering the Internet and World Wide Web as potential marketing media. Even mom and pop grocery stores are putting up Web pages and advertising them in their local markets. Driven by visions of reaching millions for a very small outlay of cash and effort, businesses are building Web sites for every imaginable product, service, and interest group. While there is nothing wrong with this, as a marketing strategy it is flawed at a basic level.

Advertising reaches out to the attention of the prospective customer. Customers have to reach out to find Internet resources. Advertising creates desires and interest; the Internet (like 1–800 phone numbers) serves that interest. In other words, your Web site is a service or information source you offer your customers rather than an advertising medium. Before you invest in the Internet, ask yourself how people will find your site and why they would want to. If you do decide to create a site, make it a value-added experience for the prospect by loading it up with as much useful and timely information as possible. These resource sites are quickly taking the place of newsletters and articles as a way of demonstrating expertise and skill to interested customers.

WORD-OF-MOUTH ADVERTISING

As the cliché goes, "Word of mouth is the best advertising." While personal recommendations are the lifeblood of most small businesses, it's important to understand that they don't come about in a vacuum. Word of mouth is a marketing tactic that you can plan and pursue with as much precision and control as any other technique covered in these pages. Good word of mouth is often a combination of publicity, networking, sales ability, advertising, and all the other marketing tools available. It comes about as the result of a synergistic combination of these various contacts. The customer sees an ad, attends a trade show, meets someone at a party, gets a recommendation, reads an article, and then calls, saying they heard about you via "word of mouth!"

The next time you hear that someone's business is 90 percent word of mouth, remember that good word of mouth is the result of many of the tactics in this book working in concert, including advertising. It is not a reason to avoid advertising. Base your decision to advertise on an evaluation of the market, the investment required, and the potential return on that investment. Set aside any sense of distaste for advertising and any feeling that your calling is somehow above the ravening crowd of advertisers. If the tool works well for your needs, it belongs in your toolbox.

CHAPTER 14

THE PHONE

In spite of all the technological advances we've seen, the telephone is still the fastest and most effective way to reach people. Everybody has one—and even if your target is away from the phone, our ubiquitous answering machines, pagers, and voice mail services have made it possible to contact anyone, anywhere, and at least deliver your message. Yet whenever I talk about using the phone as a marketing tool, I can almost feel the fear and animosity. Those awful telemarketing pitches we all live with have given telephone sales a bad rep that they don't deserve.

The phone is the single most cost-efficient marketing tool you have as a self-employed person. Even if you have no work and no money, you can use the phone to jump-start your business right now. All it takes is a plan and a phone book and the confidence to make those calls. And there's the rub.

FEAR AND "COLD" CALLING

Fear of so-called cold calling is very common and often keeps many self-employed people from using this extremely powerful marketing tool. The fear is based on fear of rejection or of being put in an unpleasant situation. Because it often involves calling strangers and asking for their attention and time, we feel uncomfortable. Yet one call can reach through barriers that letters, ads, PR, and other tools may never penetrate. In that call you can make personal contact and change prospects into people, the key to all successful marketing. You'll find out things from their attitude and tone of voice you'd never know otherwise and, if you listen, they will hand you valuable information and insights you can use over and over again. You simply cannot afford to ignore the possibilities of the phone as a marketing communications tool.

So how do you cope with fear? Start by eliminating as much uncertainty as possible by planning every aspect of your calling. This is done by getting accurate numbers and names, learning titles and pronunciations, and using a script. As unnatural as it seems, a script is the key to successful telephone prospecting. The script focuses on achieving a specific goal; it keeps you from wandering or blurting out things you don't want to say. It also saves time for both you and your prospect, something that earns respect faster than anything else you can say or do during the call.

GET THE APPOINTMENT

Before you start making calls, you must have a specific goal in mind. In general, that goal should be to get an appointment to make your sales presentation. Don't make your presentation on the phone. Let me repeat: *Do not make your sales presentation on the phone.* Don't tell everything you do, don't regale someone with references, war stories, awards you've won, or anything else. Simply tell who you are and why it's to their benefit to meet with you, and set a date and time. Then thank them and hang up. Don't offer to send a brochure or call later. Pick two or three dates and offer a choice among them. When the party turns one down, go for the next. If people say they are not interested, politely thank them and move on. Don't invest valuable energy in people who are not interested. Save it for the buyers.

DON'T TAKE IT PERSONALLY

Rejection is common in telephone sales but actual rudeness is not. If you are a low-key person, know who you're calling and why, and don't waste time; most people will hear you out. You must be relentlessly good-natured in a calm, professional way. If you're naturally perky, tone it down; if you're very serious, smile as you talk—it works wonders. When someone is rude or inconsiderate, remember the golden rule of prospecting (and life) as described in Hubert Bermont's classic, *How to be a Successful Consultant in Your own Field* (Prima Publishing, 1995): He describes a psychiatrist friend who tells him that he knows four words that would cure most of his patients if only they would take them to heart. Those four words are: *Don't Take It Personally.*

Think about it. Angry people aren't angry at you, they're angry at themselves. Mean people have to go through life miserable and friendless. If someone is tired and snaps at you when you call, it's not your fault. Don't take it personally.

USE A SCRIPT

Having a script makes it easier to avoid too much personal involvement at this stage of the game. When you call customers, you should try to put yourself in their shoes and only deal with ways you can help them. As we'll see in Chapter 17, sales is problem solving. People respond to you because you offer a solution to a problem they have. Maybe they're having a bad day and you're the first friendly voice they've spoken with. Perhaps your product or service will get them out of a dilemma they are facing.

The script itself should be simple. Introduce yourself, tell in a few words what you offer, and ask if you can get together to tell them about it. Of course, the nature of your business will determine how you handle the specifics. If you're selling a service, then you can offer to analyze their present use of similar services for free. If you have a product line, then you can offer to demonstrate it. If you sell a skill you have, ask if they use freelancers and then ask for a few minutes of their time to show them your work. If they agree to a meeting, offer several times to meet and get a specific appointment.

Another approach is to prequalify your calls by doing an informal survey. Simply call, tell them you're doing a brief survey, and ask if they will answer four or five questions. Don't do a sales pitch or go for an appointment during this call. The survey questions are designed to *qualify* them, an important part of the sales process. One effective survey script used by real estate agents goes like this:

"Mr. or Ms. [Name], please.

"Thank you. My name is [so-and-so] of [thus-and-such] Realty. I'm doing a special survey. May I ask, do you plan on moving within the next two or three years?

"May I ask, approximately when?

"Will you be staying in this area?"

If they ask why you're doing this survey, be honest. Tell them you're specializing in their neighborhood and are doing market research to determine approximately how many people will be moving and when.

This script is repeated over and over again by agents working on—*farming*—a specific area. They make a large number of calls daily for a week or two until they have reached everyone in their chosen area. At the end, they have a list of people who are considering a move and when. This list becomes their prospecting list, and the people on it will receive follow-up calls for listing appointments, newsletters about activities in their area, information packages, and bulletins telling of sales activity near their home. It's quite possible for a neophyte real estate agent to generate many years of future business with a campaign like this.

Become a Farmer

The concept of farming a specific group of prospects is valuable for any business. The farm doesn't have to be geographic; it can be an industry or interest group, or based on income, age, or other demographic profile, or it can cover any other unified target group. A survey calling campaign helps get you started and is an excellent way to start a new business or jump-start one that needs new life.

Farming works just like the real thing. You choose a fertile group with research, you till the soil by making an initial contact, you plant seeds with your marketing, and you cultivate relationships that help your farm yield plenty of steady business. It's an excellent metaphor for marketing in general, and the phone can be your primary tool in developing and harvesting your farm.

A Sample Script

Here is a simple script you can adapt to your business. Its value lies in giving you a working framework rather than a word-for-word script to use. Read it and think about how you could rework it for your business. Write out your own version and try it out loud to yourself, rewriting until it flows naturally. Then sit down with the phone and dial a number. Read through your script with the prospect. You will be nervous and your delivery probably won't win you any awards, but with practice it will get easier. The first time I did this, I was literally shaking—but I stuck with it and by the third call I had an appointment! I was literally amazed that something canned would work. That client became a friend and later said that though she knew I was nervous, she had no idea I was not talking off the cuff.

"Hello, this is Martin Edic calling for Marcia Wills. Yes, I'll hold.

"Ms. Wills, I own a local business specializing in business planning, and I wonder if I could ask you just a few short questions.

"Do you have a written business plan for your company?

(If yes:)

"Did you write it yourself or with outside help?

(If no:)

"Have you ever been asked for a plan by your banker or another business resource?

(Either way:)

"I wonder if we could get together so I could show you how an effective business plan could help your business? My clients have seen real improvements in cash flow, profits, and in some unexpected areas.

"How would Tuesday at ten o'clock work for you?

"Is Wednesday better?

"Great, I'll see you then. Thanks for your time."

A couple of things happen here. You do a little qualifying and you have two choices of where to go based on whether they have a history of using this service or not. If they do, then you can offer them an alternative resource for the service. If they have not used such a service before, asking them if they've ever needed it gives you the opportunity to get the appointment by offering a benefit they may not have considered.

ALWAYS START AT THE TOP

Because of nervousness about calling people we don't know, many of us make the mistake of calling the wrong person. Somehow it is less scary to talk to an entry-level person than to go for the top person. However, talking to people who don't have the power to make decisions is a fundamental marketing mistake, one that severely reduces the effectiveness of your campaign.

You should always aim high when seeking to do business with a company. If the company is a small business (under 100 employees, for instance), always try to reach the president or owner. If they are interested, you're talking to the right person. If they are not, ask them who in the company works with resources like you. If they give you a name, you can now call that person, introduce yourself, and say that the boss (obviously you use the name!) referred you. This means they have to at least hear you out.

If the decision maker does not have a need for your services, ask if he or she knows of anyone who might. Again, this gives you a name to drop when making that call—for instance, "Joe Mason over at Mason Brothers told me you might be interested in [whatever]." If this sounds aggressive, remember, it's your business and livelihood and this is the way a lot of business gets done. In my experience, being aggressive about something you really enjoy doing usually wins respect, as long as you know when to thank people for their time and move on.

If you deal with individuals, like home buyers, for instance, you must still seek out the decision maker before making your pitch. In Chapter 17, we'll look at ways to qualify a buyer before you go any further. As with company owners and executives, you should still ask uninterested individuals for referrals. Maybe somebody in their neighborhood or a family member needs a house or car or a new kitchen or whatever service you are selling.

JUMP-START PHONE CAMPAIGN

If you are new to being self-employed or need more business but have a limited budget, the phone can be a very powerful tool for getting things up and running quickly. The following jump-start plan works—but you must actually make every call as described. For the purposes of this plan and all cold calling, a completed call is one in which you have actually talked to the person you're seeking and either been turned down or made the contact you want. Busy signals, answering machines, and receptionist messages do not count.

- *Use your marketing plan to define your target group.* This is your farm.
- *Get a list of phone numbers, addresses, and names and put it on your computer.* Because these are unproved prospects rather than customers, your list needs to be at least 100 to 200 names—more is better. If you don't have a computer, use 3 × 5 cards and fill one out on each prospect as you get through. A card file still works!
- *Write a brief script that achieves your objective.* Set it up so that if you get to the end, you've got the appointment, issued the invitation to an event, planned the meeting, told them about your special sale, or whatever you intended to do. Practice the script out loud over the phone with several friends and revise it until it is smooth and

appealing. Make sure it has a close, a point at which you ask for specific action like an appointment. Make sure the close requires a yes or no answer.

■ *Offer an either-or choice when you close.* For instance, "Is Wednesday morning or Thursday evening better for you?" This is an assumptive close that assumes that they will respond in the affirmative. (More on closing in Chapter 17.)

■ *Get out your planner and set aside half a day every day for the next two weeks for calls.* This assumes you really need the business. This jump-start plan is work and requires a serious commitment on your part, a commitment that will be rewarded. You need a significant amount of time to gain momentum and learn to get comfortable with calling. It also takes time to get through to people. Mornings are better for business customers, late afternoon or evening for home customers.

■ *Plan on completing 20 to 50 calls per day.* This is a lot. In the future, you'll probably never need to do this many again, but now you're doing a major push and the volume will generate a lot of business.

■ *Use your planner to keep track of appointments or meetings as you make them.* Don't rush out if people are eager; schedule them in like anyone else. It adds value to appear busy and professional.

- *Have your sales presentation rehearsed and ready to go.* (See Chapter 17 for more on this.) Don't wait till you have appointments to throw together a portfolio or decide what exactly it is that you do.
- *Make the calls.* I know it is hard and scary but nothing you can do will do more for your business, especially if things are slow. And you'll learn more about sales and marketing and your business in the next two weeks than any course, class, or advisor could teach you.

This jump-start plan is tough, but it works. Staying motivated is the challenge—especially if you're getting rejected regularly. I've found that a little perspective change can help. For example, if you make 20 calls to get an appointment that results in $100 worth of profit for you (a very conservative percentage), then each of those 20 calls put $5 in your pocket. Set an hourly rate if you like. Want to make $50 per hour? Complete 10 calls.

This numbers game actually underestimates the value of each call—the right new customer should be worth much more in future business and referrals. As a writer, I found that even the smallest client netted me several hundred dollars per year. In my recording studio, the average project brings in several thousand dollars, making cold calling a much warmer proposition.

DAILY PHONE ETIQUETTE

Phones are more than prospecting tools. You spend a lot of time on the phone, and it is the primary way others reach you. The way you answer the phone and receive and record messages, your response time, and your accessibility all have a major effect on the success of your business. I feel that one of the biggest advantages self-employed people have over their bigger competition is accessibility and response time. Because you handle everything, you can make quick decisions and you can let people reach you directly if you choose.

One of the trade-offs in choosing self-employment is how available you are to your customers. For many of us, every day can be a workday and every hour a work hour. We don't work nine to five, Monday through Friday. This is a big shock to those fleeing corporate life for the challenge of self-employment. Fortunately, we can also be flexible, taking off weekdays on short notice, working odd hours and being off odd hours, and choosing how hard we need to work. We may kill ourselves for a week on a profitable rush job and take several days off the next week.

This same flexibility has a downside when it comes to accessibility. Without an office staff to field calls when we're away, we risk the possibility of missing business we want. This leads to what novelist Lawrence Durrell described as the journalist's affliction: The feeling that somewhere, right now, there was something going on that they were missing. Today, I see many of my self-employed friends suffering from a similar twitch when they are away from their phones and pagers.

Being easy to reach is a significant marketing advantage. Take advantage of the numerous options in telecommunications and make it easy for people to reach you even when you're on your way to day care or sunning yourself on the beach. Cell phones, pagers, voice mail, and other gadgets make this possible. If you don't want to be tethered to a phone, check your messages frequently and always respond immediately, no matter where you are. Nothing is more frustrating than reaching an answering machine that promises instant response and then hearing nothing. People who do not return messages do not get my business. It's that simple.

The way you answer the phone is important because it helps convey that vital positive first impression. Be alert, smile, and identify yourself personally when you answer. Don't say: "Edic Wells Associates" say: "Edic Wells Associates, this is Martin Edic." Never answer the phone rudely; you don't know who is calling. It could be a new customer ready to spend serious money.

Don't use your home phone line if you work at home. In my experience, companies are so used to home offices that there is no stigma attached to working out of your house as long as you are professional. A separate line means your kids don't answer the phone, your answering machine has its own business-oriented message, and the background noise is in your office and not the rec room. Sound professional and you are professional to your caller.

Be accessible for all necessary forms of communications. This means buying a fax machine and a modem for your computer, along with the requisite separate phone line. Get a 1-800 number if you do business out of state. It is a bargain and a courtesy to your customers. Have an e-mail account and use it. E-mail is rapidly becoming a primary channel for business communications, especially when you can attach files and send your work across the planet in a snap.

The phone is today's communications device. This will change; it may not be long before we meet in virtual conference rooms with clients from all over the planet. But the value of one-on-one, real-time conversation will stay the same. When you're there with a person, even via wires, you can make an impression (positive or negative), iron out objections, offer solutions, elaborate on details, and *communicate*. And that is what all marketing aims to accomplish. In the next chapter, we're going to look at getting face to face in the real world through networking and good old-fashioned schmoozing.

CHAPTER 15

FACE-TO-FACE PROSPECTING: NETWORKING

You're in a large room, perhaps a banquet hall, filled with people in business dress, wandering about waiting for the evening's events to start. Here and there you see groups speaking animatedly about what appear to be serious and absorbing business concerns. In your pocket, ready for a deft pass, is a wad of your freshly minted business cards. You scan the room anxiously and, with relief, spot a casual acquaintance. As you wend your way toward each other, a polyester-clad figure suddenly appears with hand outstretched. "Charley Smith from Exeter Insurance. We met at [some place you may not remember]." Congratulations, you're networking.

This nightmare takes place all over the world as earnest Chambers of Commerce and other business organizations sponsor what they fondly call *networking events,* places where people like yourself can schmooze, drink overpriced drinks, listen to a hired motivational speaker, and exchange business cards. The goal is to enhance the local business climate and offer members a chance to talk about their wares. The reality is a room full of corporate salespeople and business owners from a random selection of companies all engaged in an artificial ritual. These cliché networking events have turned many self-employed people off to the whole concept of networking. Yet networking, or creative schmoozing as I prefer to think of it, is a vital and potentially potent marketing tactic.

Are you good at walking into a room full of strangers and casually starting conversations that lead to profitable business? If your answer is no, you're like most of us. However, if that room is full of people who fit your customer profile to a tee, know you or of you, and have a personal interest in your abilities, it gets a lot easier. And that brings me to the point of this diatribe: Most networking gets done in exactly the wrong places with the wrong group of people.

GO WHERE THE CUSTOMERS ARE

The number one, apparently obvious but oft-ignored rule of networking is: *Go where the customers are.* Yet we tend to join organizations whose members do what we do and know what we know—in other words, whose members are our competition. As a writer, I might find it interesting to attend a writers' conference—but it would undoubtedly be more profitable to attend an editors' conference. A self-employed home remodeler is far better off at a home show than at a builder's association meeting, and a consultant should be hanging out with groups of potential clients rather than other consultants. Go where the customers are.

YOU ARE AN EXPERT

Rule number two of effective networking is *you are an expert.* This may seem daunting, but the fact is that as a self-employed person you are an expert. It says so when you hand out a business card that says: Jane Doe, Business Planning (substitute your profession). But being an expert and being recognized as an expert are two different things. Recognition comes from experience, referrals, word of mouth, publicity, advertising, and most of the tactics covered in this book. Once others begin to see you as an expert, networking becomes a much more interesting and effective marketing tactic.

But what if you are not a recognized expert? Start by using your marketing plan to generate recognition. Publicity is usually the first step; we'll look at this vital tactic in detail in Chapter 16. Even an announcement of your new status as a self-employed person is a start. Any publications you have written for, interesting projects or clients you've worked with, or educational experience you have can act as icebreakers in networking situations.

PLAN YOUR NETWORKING

Like all marketing tactics, networking is most effective when you have a plan. A simple networking plan may consist of joining two or three associations or organizations that reflect the interests of your customers, attending trade shows and seminars related to your customers' needs, and getting involved in community projects and promotions that put you in contact with local business people. Even if you run a neighborhood retail store, you can join your local merchants' group, get active in local activities like festivals and neighborhood associations, and sign on as a sponsor for events in schools. These things take time and energy—but the return is generous because most of us like to do business with people we know and respect.

MEETING THE KEY PLAYERS

Merely joining and attending is not enough. Your plan should include a list of key players in your business, people you would like to get to know. These key people tend to be at the center of every industry and interest group. They know everyone and often serve as the facilitators for many of the insider deals that newcomers witness from outside. Developing a key people list often means asking questions, listening, and observing for a while at the beginning of your contact with a group. Find out who knows everyone and introduce yourself to them. Simply tell them who you are, what you do, that you're new to the group or organization, and that you'd like to help out in any way you can.

This approach underscores another important aspect of networking: You must give before you receive. If a conversation comes around to a subject close to your area of expertise, offer your valued input without making a pitch. If you see an article on a subject of interest to one of your key people, send it to him or her with a brief personal note. If you hear about an exciting new business or event one of your prospective customers is involved with, tell your key people about it. Try to get to know media writers and reporters in your business. Every business has its own experts and trade publications, and most of them thrive by knowing everyone. Meet them and keep them informed when you run into something interesting or newsworthy.

THE SMALL TOWN MODEL

All of this may have a familiar ring to those of you who grew up in a small town or tightly knit city neighborhood. These places always have movers and shakers who run things, know everyone, and keep track of everything everyone is doing. Recommendations and referrals are the way things get done. Your area of business is no different from a small town. After a few years of attending trade shows and association meetings or reading the trades, you'll be part of that small town dynamic. That's where the real networking occurs.

My first two books were written for professional woodworkers. My brother owns a cabinet-making business, and his shop was in a large industrial loft building shared by numerous small businesses including several woodshops. As a marketing consultant, I naturally ended up talking about marketing and the woodworking business when I joined my brother for lunch at a restaurant near the building. Gradually I got to know the ins and outs of the woodworking life by meeting woodworkers, sharing war stories, and handing out quite a bit of free advice. Eventually that advice became a business book for woodworkers, soon followed by another, both published by the publisher of several magazines and many books aimed at woodworkers. And I found myself an expert in an area I never suspected existed.

GIVE A SEMINAR OR SPEECH

Your expertise or specialization, when recognized, makes it a lot easier to join in on conversations and meet new potential customers. If you are Jane Doe, Business Planner, you can start by writing for your local business paper about business planning or offering a free seminar on planning. Although this may seem like giving away the farm, it is usually the opposite that is true. Many readers and attendees are really seeking expert help rather than do-it-yourself knowledge. They will approach you or be receptive to your marketing after you've given them evidence of your abilities. Even those who do it themselves often make referrals.

Seminars and classes are a great way to market yourself that can be adapted to almost any business. Run a health food store? Give an afternoon lecture on new developments in vitamin supplements. Install computer networks? A seminar on designing facilities for future networking needs may net you lucrative contracts. Do you have a craft or art you pursue? Classes on techniques or business practices can lead to sales.

Producing a seminar or lecture has gotten much easier because they are so popular that many organizations are always on the lookout for speakers and presenters. Put together a proposal for a short seminar and propose it to organizations whose members are likely prospects. Offer your services for free or for a donation to a charity of your choice. Reserve the right to hand out marketing materials or make back-of-room sales if appropriate. This approach often means that the sponsoring company or organization will handle the production of the event, including supplying a site, public address system, refreshments, seating, and other details. They will usually do some marketing, but you should plan your own marketing support if the event is open to the public. Use press releases and other publicity to get the word out. And don't forget to call everyone on your list and issue a personal invitation.

Seminars for Profit

You can run for-profit seminars as an adjunct business. In most cities, it is possible to rent a conference room at a small business center, school, or hotel. Bear in mind that you'll have to handle a lot of the details yourself and it will be your responsibility to advertise the event. Often these events only generate a small profit—but they can mean a lot of business and an increase in your expert status.

Seminars require a lot of resources and planning. If you're charging for them, it helps to be a recognized expert already so that your name attracts attendees. Even if you charge a significant amount, it can be challenging to make a profit unless you make seminars your business and run them regularly, taking advantage of having done all the work for the first one.

To really profit from seminars you must have something additional to sell to attendees. This can include books, tapes, software, and other information items. Often a product is featured as part of a seminar. These include diverse items like planners, exercise equipment, mutual funds, and other items. You have to make sure that you go beyond the sales pitch and offer some real value, even if attendees don't end up buying your product.

From a marketing and networking point of view, seminars work best as a way to demonstrate your abilities and build customer relationships. They work particularly well for subjects that require general training followed by a potential for offering a customized solution. For instance, you may offer a training seminar on a particular software program and then pitch your services as a consultant to come in and install a customized version of that program for individual participants. The real profit in this type of seminar is the long-term business it generates.

My accountant takes a similar approach. He offers to come in and set up a popular money management program on his clients' computers. They can then bring the files in each spring at tax time, and he can instantly import them into his system and do their tax returns. He saves time, and they don't have to go through the agonizing process of assembling all their records each year. I've suggested he take the process to the next logical step: Offer his clients a seminar on retirement planning using the software to track portfolios and mutual funds. Because he offers financial planning and mutual fund sales, this would give him an excellent opportunity to turn his "tax return only" clients into full-service clients. He might even consider giving away the software package (a $40 item) as an incentive.

NETWORKING IS NOT FREE

Networking is not free advertising. In fact, it can be quite expensive. Like all of these tactics, it must be evaluated in terms of the overall long-term return on your investment. That trade show in Las Vegas may seem out of your league, but it can create contacts you'd never make in Kansas. I'm reminded of two graphic designers who watched with a little envy as a friend in the same business carved out a very lucrative niche for himself specializing in ads for pro audio manufacturers. When they asked him how he found his clients, he told them to attend the annual trade show on the other side of the country and to take their portfolio from booth to booth for the whole weekend. He assured them that with their excellent book they'd snag at least one or two new clients worth thousands in interesting and profitable work. Their response was typical: attending the show would cost them $2,000 and they couldn't afford it. They didn't go, and they will never know if the investment would have paid off. However, their friend, a recognized expert in the field, was sure it would have, so I believe they missed out on an important opportunity. The long-term potential almost certainly far outweighed the cost.

HAVE FAITH IN HUMAN NATURE

An important part of that story may be the unsaid part. Perhaps the two designers were uncomfortable with the idea of going out and pitching their work to strangers. An important part of networking is diving in. You have to make the effort, no matter how nervous or foolish you may feel about it. Everyone faces these moments, and most of us are sympathetic to the plight of newcomers. Find friendly faces, talk a little shop, and pick their brains. Ask for advice and introductions. My last secret of networking is the best one: People love to help out other people, especially when they are approached as a mentor or guide. It not only makes them feel good, it increases their value among their contemporaries and peers. Have you ever watched a group of people gather around someone seeking directions in a strange city? They are all vying for the opportunity to help someone they don't know.

This desire to interact and help each other is a fundamental part of networking. Humans are communal and sociable creatures. When we meet new friends, we make an untested investment in them. We spend our time and reputation on them because we take an interest in their success. If they fail us or lose our trust, we will be wary the next time. As you achieve a degree of success, remember those who helped you and do as they did once for you. When you see newbies hanging out in the corner at a function, introduce yourself and shepherd them around a bit. They may turn out to be your best prospect as both a business source and a resource.

NETWORKING MEANS TAKING PART

Ultimately, the real secret of networking is participation. Get involved with every aspect of your business life. Take classes. Go to community events. Volunteer at nonprofit organizations. Join the board of directors of an organization. Get yourself onto committees and actively participate. Like every tactic in this book, networking does not happen in a vacuum. You must reach out and take an action before others do. Leaders are often those who just can't stand inertia: They may not be any more skilled or vivacious than anyone else—they just don't like waiting. You can become one just by going for it. And when you do, you'll suddenly find others right behind you, supporting your effort.

CHAPTER 16

PUBLICITY

Publicity is an exceptionally effective, low-cost marketing tactic useful to any self-employed person. It's effective because the printed or broadcast word has more respectability and believability when it is editorial than when it is advertising. *Editorial* is that part of a publication or broadcast program that represents (allegedly) objective content. It includes everything that is not paid for and whose content is not controlled by an advertiser. Because most media companies take pains to separate editorial decision making from the influence of advertisers, editorial content has more credibility with the audience. In other words, a complimentary article about you is worth more than an ad you buy.

PUBLIC RELATIONS VERSUS PUBLICITY

Because of this enhanced credibility, most large companies spend considerable sums on professional public relations firms or in-house PR offices. These pros swamp the media with press releases and announcements of events, new products, and personnel changes. They create and produce promotional events and handle media-oriented crisis management when things go awry. Chances are the "official spokesperson" you hear on the news when a company has problems is a public relations professional. These aspects of the PR game (events and damage control) are not usually relevant to the needs of the self-employed businessperson. For that reason, I'm focusing on one aspect of public relations: *publicity.*

GETTING GOOD PRESS

Getting good press is the goal of your publicity efforts. While there is a school of thought that says any publicity is good publicity, I disagree, particularly when you're the only employee of the enterprise getting the bad press. You cannot rectify bad situations by firing the responsible person or promising to get to the bottom of the scandal "no matter what it takes." Everyone knows that you did it or has the perception that you did. So we're going to stick with getting good press.

Anyone who has worked for any public media company knows how many people there are trying to get media attention. Press releases, information packets, and phone calls pour in every day. And, while many of them can be almost absurdly unnewsworthy, a surprising amount of the news you read and hear is generated by these publicity efforts. In fact, it has been estimated that as much as 90 percent of the news comes from these sources! And they're not just sources—many media editors with limited staff writers will use press releases verbatim, pulling headlines and body copy directly from the PR writer's work.

Creating Publicity the Press Can Use

The keys to successful publicity reside in understanding the needs of the press. First, they have a ravenous and unending need for more news. Remember—it's called the news because it is new. That means that any publicity you send has a chance of getting read by an editor and at least considered for publication. The second need they have is for news that is relevant to their readers' interests. Editors will tell you that they get zillions of press releases for stories that are totally inappropriate for their audience (and in some crackpot cases, inappropriate for any media). Your publicity efforts, like all your marketing, are much more effective when you target your media. This means choosing media that share a common interest with your customers and only sending them publicity that deals with those interests.

TELL A COMPELLING STORY

A third important consideration in getting press is having a newsworthy story. The key word here is *story*. An announcement of a new product is not news until you tell why and how that product will affect the lives of the readers. By the same token, an announcement that you are now in business for yourself seldom generates more than a single line of news because it's not news unless someone has an emotional connection to it.

News contains something new of interest to the readers. The key words here are *new* and *interest*. Sending a press release out announcing your existence a year after you open your business is not news, it's old. Your publicity efforts must be timely, and it often helps to tie them in with some event occurring at the same time. A new nightclub might choose to open on the weekend the city is hosting a music conference. You may offer a seminar on the Internet in conjunction with a new service provider opening its doors or the local school system going online. The connection makes it newsworthy.

You must also offer something of interest or benefit to the readers. Where the school system is going online, you might offer a course for parents so they can keep up with what their kids are learning. I guarantee you you'd get good coverage by linking the two together and offering a real needed service as part of your story.

MAKE A LOCAL CONNECTION

The final criterion for getting the attention of editors is *use local names;* the more the better. Although at first glance dropping names may seem like a gimmick, it results in good press because people like to feel connected with their community—and seeing or hearing the names of people they know builds that connection. This is not restricted to your local media. Communities are not just geographic, they also center around shared interests. People develop local reputations within their interest groups as well as within their locale. A major goal of any publicity is to build your reputation within the interest groups that your customers are members of. Like networking, your publicity must go where the customers are.

Dropping names is easier when you have quotes from satisfied customers, positive comments by insiders, participation in projects by associations and groups, and proof of your involvement in the community. If you teach or consult on a current model based on the work of others like the Total Quality Management craze we all witnessed in recent years, you can quote from their words to support your press release. For instance, a TQM trainer might headline a new business announcement with a compelling quote from Edward Deming, the founder of TQM. This gets a familiar name into your news even if you're not personally acquainted.

You can also ask noted friends or clients for their comments or quotes. You may even include a pseudo-interview with yourself, filling your publicity with fascinating quotes and stories from the president of your company. This can lead to requests for interviews and for your opinion on breaking news, both of which will contribute to your stature and expert reputation.

PUTTING TOGETHER A PRESS RELEASE

Writing a press release can follow a format. Unless you are an experienced news writer, I suggest you start out by following the classic formula. Its structure is the same as that followed by journalists, and that makes it easier for an editor to take it as is and use it. The goal of all these guidelines is to make your publicity easy for a busy editor to absorb and use. Like any sales-related effort, this is solving a problem—in this case, helping the media provide newsworthy information for their readers.

The formula for formatting and writing a press release is simple. Double-space your text and use wide margins so that the editor can do an edit directly on your release. Use a plain serif typeface or font and avoid the temptation to insert graphics, use colored paper, or add other attention-getting gimmicks. Goofy press releases are not "unusual and eye-catching," they are common and usually the sign of an amateur. Be businesslike. Besides, plain paper and text are much easier to read, a major consideration to someone who wades through mountains of print every day.

On your businesslike letterhead, on the left margin, type (in caps) FOR IMMEDIATE RELEASE and put the date either below it or on the opposite margin. Then, on the next line type Contact: and your name and contact info. Go one third down the page and center your headline. Like your ads and direct mail, your publicity needs a catchy headline that draws attention and tells the story. The headline is the first and most important part of your press release. A great headline always attracts editors' attention because they write heads all day. Write a good one and you may see it in print.

Headlines That Attract Attention

What makes a good head? It tells the story and why the reader would want to read it. If you're an information systems manager and you see a story in a trade magazine titled "Untangling the Wires and the People Who Use Them: How Networking Consultants Helped One Company Get Connected," you'd read it. It addresses several problems you face daily and offers the promise of a solution. Your head should try to tell the basics: what, who, where, when, how, and why. You won't get all of them in, but make sure the relevant ones are covered.

The Subhead

The sample headline in the previous section uses another important component of storytelling: a subhead.

A subhead simply elaborates on the catchiness of the headline by providing a brief fillip of information. It also helps you cover more of the who, what, and where without turning your headline into an opus. Subheads get read—so use them unless your main headline is so compelling it's not necessary. You can capitalize your head and then use initial caps in your subhead to set them apart.

The First Paragraph

The classic structure for news is a pyramid with the important information heading the article and the writer gradually working down into the details as the copy proceeds. News gets written this way because the pros assume that most readers only read the first few lines or paragraphs of an article. The further you go, the more readers drop off, so you focus the meat of your message at the top. As a result, your first paragraph really tells the whole story in broad, compelling strokes, followed by paragraphs addressing details in order of importance.

Skip down to the halfway point on the page and start your first paragraph. The first paragraph should cover all of the who, what, where, and so on again, in more detail. It should focus on the most exciting, profitable, timely, and compelling aspects of the story. It is a good place to insert a clever quote from yourself or another expert. (By the way, don't write press releases in the first person; write them as though you are an enthusiastic news writer covering the story. Then quote yourself. It's easy because you can make up the quotes you need!) The style should be upbeat, stressing the potential of your information rather than focusing on negativity. One exception to this would be if you choose to put a frightening scenario in the opener and then demonstrate how your business resolves it.

Follow-up paragraphs tell more, drop names, and offer resources for more information. Real-world examples and stories of how other customers have benefited from your business are effective, as are stories of how you acquired your expertise or experience. Keep the overall release brief, not more than two pages. If you need to include more information, write a separate fact sheet. This fact sheet can give biographical information, if relevant, capabilities info, references, and so on. You can also include photos, brochures, articles, press releases about your business, and other info, which when assembled in a folder becomes a *press kit*. (More on press kits later.)

The final paragraph should wrap up by addressing the basics again. This fits the classic speech formula in which you tell the audience what you are going to tell them, tell them, and then tell them what you told them. This repetition is only effective if you have unique details, experiences, and anecdotes for each retelling. Otherwise it becomes filler and won't fool an experienced reader.

Finish off your release by typing ### or -33- and centering it below the last paragraph. These are journalistic conventions that tell the editor that the article is finished and no more pages follow. Proofread your writing, spell check it, and then have someone else do the same. Mistakes will not enamor you to editors.

Once again, keep it brief. No more than two pages is the rule. If the editor wants to know more, you'll get a call—that's what the contact info is for.

Finding an Angle

Once you've learned to write a simple press release, you can use it whenever you have a really newsworthy development in your business. Keep your mind open to the newsworthiness of your life as a self-employed person. Like a reporter, you should always be looking for an angle or slant that makes an otherwise mundane story interesting. Put yourself in the reader's shoes. For example, have you figured out a unique way to incorporate your child's day care regimen into your business life? Telling how could generate press that not only attracts attention to your problem-solving abilities but tells the world what you do. Other angles are unique clients, weird problems, unusual success stories, overcoming adversity, breaking into new markets, breakthrough products, interesting niche businesses, and case studies of projects you've done. One good way to define a good story is when someone you know or work with finds it interesting.

YOUR MEDIA LIST

In Chapter 12, we looked at creating a client list. To successfully promote your business through publicity, you need a good media list. Fortunately, it is not hard to assemble one—start at your local library. Go to the reference desk and enlist a knowledgeable reference librarian to help you uncover relevant directories and media sources. Larger libraries also have extensive online resources and CD-ROM databases you can search by subject. Your own Internet connections can also generate numerous lists. Narrow the lists down to media that your target markets pay attention to, including trade magazines, Web sites, newsletters, radio programs (rather than stations), TV producers of relevant programming, talk shows, and other targeted media. If you serve a local business or retail market, use all your local media.

Get Current Names

As you assemble your list, get current names for every media outlet. With publications, try to identify the features, business, or general editor depending on your story. You might target a release about that day care situation to both a features editor and a business editor. Call the media office and double-check the name of the current person holding the position before you send out your release. An accurately spelled name is important. Mail to all of your media list every time you send a release—you don't want one editor to feel you offered your story to another as an exclusive. An exception would be if you had a really newsworthy exclusive and wanted to repay a favor or incur one.

Get Current Fax Numbers— and Broadcast to Them

When I purchased a fax modem for my computer, it came with software that made it easy for me to automate my publicity distribution. I called everyone on my media list and got current fax numbers, which I entered into a minidatabase within the fax software. Now when I want to send out a press release, I compose it on my computer and tell the fax software to send it in the background. It personalizes each cover page, dials until it gets through, and sends all the releases automatically. Most media are used to receiving publicity via fax and will route it to the person it is addressed to. This is a great example of how computers and sophisticated broadcast-capable fax machines can really save you time and money.

Keep Track of Publication Schedules

Send your press releases out far enough ahead to fit each publication's schedule. Monthly magazines often work months ahead of publication dates, while radio is almost daily in its choices. Print media have a longer lead time than broadcast media. Pick the publication deadline and get your release there early enough to follow up with a call before it's too late. Scheduling your releases is vital; it is easy to miss a deadline and not get coverage for a dated event or announcement.

Follow-Up Calls Get You Out of the Slush Pile

Follow-up telephone calls are vital. Often, your call is what gets your releases dragged out of the pile on a busy desktop and into consideration. In addition, your personal contact puts a voice and personality into your information. Keep your calls brief and to the point. Don't waste time; these people are always working on a busy deadline schedule. Simply call and tell them you're following up on your press release. Ask them if they got it (if they didn't, offer to immediately fax one to them), ask if they have any questions, and then shut up and listen. They'll tell you if they need anything. In my experience, 90 percent of the time they'll be reading your release as they speak to you, a valuable lesson in why follow-up is so important.

MAKING INTERVIEWS COUNT

If someone wants an interview as a result of your efforts, make yourself available. Being interviewed can be a frustrating experience—many interviewers know nothing about you or what you do. They're simply responding to the unrelenting demand for content they face every day. To make interviews count, you need to prepare yourself by rehearsing, having a punchlist of points you want to make in front of you, and by actually preparing questions for the interviewer. As odd as this seems, many interviewers will use your questions! After all, you are the expert and know what's interesting about what you do. (In theory, anyway. I've heard many interviews where the alleged experts were so close to the subject matter that they could not step back and make it interesting to an outsider. This is an excellent argument for rehearsing with a friend—preferably one who knows nothing about your business.)

Prepare a background information kit if you are seeking a lot of interviews and send it or fax it when you are asked for an interview. This kit will really win you brownie points with writers and talk show hosts, who routinely have to wing it unprepared for interviews. Your brief but cogent package of info can make them sound good—which makes you sound good. If you're selling a product or service via a 1-800 number or e-mail address, get the interviewer's permission to announce it regularly during the interview. Rather than a sales pitch you can simply say: "For more information call 1-800-000-0000."

Once you've done a few interviews, you'll develop a routine that helps you get through the process and ensures that you get to the info you want to convey. Notes and experience really help. If you get stage fright, remember to take a few deep breaths, think of the interview as a conversation with someone who is interested in what you do, be yourself, and pretend that stage fright only lasts until the moment you're on. After that you go for it.

Using a Press Kit

Use coverage and interviews to get more coverage. Assemble a press kit with information, photos, samples, press clippings, and a list of media appearances. Put it into a nice folder and make up a pile of them so that you can get one out on a moment's notice. Keep it up to date. When you have a lot of stuff in there, weed out aged or irrelevant information and focus on the best stories and exposure you've received.

Sending Your Customers Your Publicity Info

Remember your customer list and your regular mailings to it? Send out press releases to your customers as well as to the media. This is an excellent way to keep them involved in what you do, who you're working with, and new products or services you offer. In addition to sending out press releases, you can send out clippings of any interesting coverage you receive. It may seem like tooting your own horn—but keeping your customers abreast of what you do not only keeps you on their A lists, it also gets them invested in your success. Most of us like to see people we like and respect succeed.

LOCAL EXPERT STATUS

Getting good publicity is a gradual process. When you've got a great story, it's easy. When your announcement is more run of the mill you may get a mention or nothing. However, editors are always looking for stories; after they have read about you several times, they may find an angle you didn't see and generate a story from it. Eventually, they'll come to think of you as a local expert on your subject and will call and ask for commentary or background when your interest area is in the news. This can lead to requests for public speaking engagements and other opportunities to create exposure for your business.

Becoming a local expert doesn't have to happen gradually. Have you ever wondered why certain people seem to get interviewed and quoted in the media all the time? They may have set out to establish themselves as experts. Most reporters and editors keep a tickler file of sources for every kind of information imaginable. One effective tactic is to send them a rotary file card or 3 × 5 card with your contact information and a list of areas you have experience with. Include a letter letting them know you're available if they ever need a source on these subjects.

A local business planner I know used this tactic to position herself as an expert on start-ups, small business financing, business planning, market planning, and work-

ing with the local banking community. Her name
appears repeatedly in articles about new companies,
start-ups, getting loans, and similar matters. And she usually gets identified as a specialist in start-up business
planning as part of the deal.

Does this all sound like the news is a fixed game
created by clever marketing and PR people? My
personal experience tells me that—like all things in
life—the answer is sometimes yes and sometimes no.
The more respected the media the more likely they
are to check on stories, use multiple sources, and pub-
lish because a story is newsworthy. They know how
the publicity machine works and view it as one way
to generate news. They also have a stake in the success
of their community, their advertisers, and their business area, so running stories that illustrate that success
is of benefit to them. Less scrupulously reporting news
reporters are often hampered by a lack of money,
different editorial goals, and a closer relationship
between advertising sales and editorial departments.
They will often print anything you send them if you
advertise. Most will vehemently deny any connection—but it is often there. I've had advertising space
people offer my clients articles in issues that they
purchase ads in. My recommendation? Take the article if you feel you should advertise there, but realize
that savvy readers of these publications know the score
and take the articles with a grain of salt. It probably

won't hurt you, but it won't have the impact of the real, unadulterated thing.

I learned how to work a low-budget publicity campaign as a member of a rock band in my twenties. We quickly learned what got our shows coverage and what didn't, who to call and who to put on the guest list, which media pulled in a crowd and which didn't make a difference. We learned about press kits and the power of a good, entertaining, current photo. We also learned that writers keep files on people they cover regularly, that offering to take someone to lunch after you've had several contacts is often a good idea, and— most important—that you ultimately have to be very good at what you do to get good coverage. Those lessons made me respect the power of the press but also taught me that the press exist to help us as much as we exist to help them—and that you'll meet some very interesting and devoted people in the process.

CHAPTER 17

SELLING YOURSELF

Every tactic we've covered thus far has had one objective: To get you in touch with prospective customers and give you the opportunity to turn them into current customers for your products or services. That opportunity may take the form of an appointment to present a portfolio of work or experience, the chance to make a presentation to a group, an invitation to provide a quote or estimate, or an enticement to get a buyer into your store or place of business. Whatever situation your business requires, you are now face to face with prospects and have the opportunity to sell to them. It took a lot of effort to get them here; now you must capitalize on it.

Most small business experts, when asked about the essential skill required for success as a self-employed person, would answer: "The ability to sell." Selling is where the essence of marketing comes into focus. That essence, which pervades everything covered in this book, is communication. You market to establish a link with customers. You use sales to create an interchange that benefits both parties. In other words, the hallmarks of successful sales are communication and a mutually beneficial transaction. Getting there is one of the most interesting challenges faced by any business owner.

THE FEAR AND THE MYSTERY

Mystery and fear are associated with selling. The average person seldom considers themself an effective salesperson. To describe yourself as a sales pro is to invite an undercurrent of distrust in our society. This prejudice dates back to the class distinctions between the landed nobility and the merchants of feudal times. It feeds off the cliché of a salesperson as a fast-talking, glad-handing dinosaur with an insincere smile and a mouth full of lies. This image of a salesperson is far from reality. In reality, salespeople are often among the most attentive and honorable people in a business; they know that lies leave long and unpleasant memories. Because they work on an incentive or commission basis they are, in fact, entrepreneurs. They are also listeners, counselors, consultants, experts, and business partners. They perform the most essential task of capitalism—

making the deal. And they are often among the most highly compensated people in large companies.

The mystery of selling comes because we seldom have the chance to learn anything about how to sell. We don't learn it in business schools, and what we learn on the street is often laced with lore and moxie that can kill a deal. The fear comes from being placed in a situation where we must tell the world that we are great and that people should pay to participate in our greatness. If they say no, we typically experience anger, rejection, depression, and lowered self-esteem. The only way out of this extreme emotional reaction to sales is to understand selling as a process that anyone can learn and apply.

POSITIVE SELLING

It helps to consider the enormous potential of learning to sell. Selling generates business, cements positive relationships, weeds out poor prospects, teaches us about human nature, and offers us ample opportunities to meet new people. As a self-employed person, you are truly selling what you believe in (if you aren't, you should seriously reevaluate your line of work). Selling becomes much easier when you are enthusiastic about what you do and what you have to offer.

In approaching a sales situation, you have two choices of how to go about it. You can sell on the positive merits of the situation, or you can sell on the

negative aspects of not making the deal. Both work—
but the negative approach has one thing going against
it. As I noted earlier, we process negative information
by creating an image and then negating it. This means
that when you use a negative example or consequence
to create a sale, prospects must act out that negative
consequence in their heads before they get to the
positive effect of completing the transaction. They may
buy—but they will have a lingering negative feeling
about the entire transaction, which may keep them
from doing repeat business.

SELLING IS A PROCESS

This chapter constitutes a mini-course in the basics of
selling for self-employed people. For much greater detail on the subject, see the companion book in this
series, *Sales for the Self-Employed*. The mini-course is a
six-step process that takes you from initial contact to
follow-up after the sale. The most important thing you
can learn here is to stick to the process and make sure
you cover each step every time you sell. When things
are not working or get out of control, it usually means
you've skipped a step. I find that it helps to actually
write down the steps on a 3 × 5 card and refer to it as
you go through the process, mentally checking off each
step as you complete it.

If you encounter extreme hostility, indifference, or
a clear lack of motivation on the part of the buyer, don't

spend a lot of time trying to turn the situation around. It is not an efficient use of your time to try to turn a clear no into a yes. It probably will not happen and you will have wasted time you could have spent working with someone who really wants your services.

The first step in the process is a simple yet critical one: Meeting your prospect face to face at the beginning of a sales presentation.

Step One: Meet and Greet

You've arranged to meet a potential customer at his office to tell him about your consulting services. You've agreed upon a time and day, and your contact has blocked out one hour for your meeting, starting at 10 A.M. You get a late start, quickly gather up your presentation materials, jump in the car, realize that you forgot the address, and finally get to his office five minutes late and feeling a little disheveled. Your contact offers coffee and you accept, which means another five minutes of fiddling around while someone serves the coffee. Finally you get down to business.

Congratulations. You've blown the meet-and-greet stage of the sales process. No matter how good a job you do from here on in, you cannot erase the initial impression you've made of being somewhat disorganized and slightly unreliable, and maybe a time waster as well. The fact that your prospect made it clear that he blocked out a period of time for your meeting should have told you that time was a very important commodity for him—and getting started on time, an important consideration.

Making a good first impression is important because you can never go back and do it over again. You can return to the other steps in this process and re-evaluate them, but meeting and greeting is a one-time thing. For this reason it is especially important to plan your meeting and prepare ahead. Your appearance, tone of voice, handshake, organization, and general attitude are all important. Dress one step up from the level of your prospects for the first meeting. This means emulating their style but going just a little more formal. It does not necessarily imply a business suit; in fact, there are many times when a suit will be a turnoff. I remember seeing a young kitchen designer show up on a muddy construction site for a client meeting in heels and an expensive suit. She literally could not do the required walk-through of the project and lost out on the job.

Your voice should be clear, alert, and responsive. Don't mutter, cover your mouth with your hands, or turn away from your customer when you talk. Speak eye to eye and smile when you introduce yourself. Smiling does something almost indefinable to your entire demeanor. Stand up straight and shake hands firmly. If your customer offers one of those contest handshakes, meet the pressure but don't get involved in a strength test.

Organize yourself mentally and physically before your meeting. Mental organization can be a rehearsal or simply going over a checklist of what you know about these people, their business, and their personal interests along with what you hope to accomplish. Physical organization includes having your materials or presentation in perfect order so you don't fumble or lose things, having fresh business cards at hand to distribute, doing a check in the mirror before you meet, and brushing your teeth before you leave your office.

This preparation for meeting should become a habit, as should arriving early. Always arrive five or ten minutes early and make it clear that you are not in a hurry if they apologize for running late themselves. If you are waiting in a reception area, have some small task with you that you can easily pull out and do, like making notes or working in your planner. Don't talk on the phone; you want to be free at once when you meet your prospect.

The final aspect of the meet-and-greet step is *full attention and concentration.* You must be completely immersed in the moment during a sales meeting. Developing the ability to put aside other mental activity to focus on the needs and messages of your customer is what sets sales professionals apart from neophytes. Be completely there and take a real interest in what you are doing. Listen from the first minute you enter the arena. Keep your antennae out as soon as you enter any sales situation. I cannot count how many times I've learned something interesting about clients just from sitting in their reception areas and observing. You can learn about their business style, how well things are going, whether your prospect is busy or has extra time, and even whether they are a person or company you want to do business with. Sometimes you'll catch a vibe that warns you to keep your eyes open. Don't ignore these signals.

So you are in the room, you've met, made a few minutes of small talk to loosen things up, and now it's time to get started. Many of us make a basic error here by starting off with a discussion of what we do. Block that impulse and get ready for step two, the step that will tell you everything you need to know to move the sales process ahead: Qualifying your customer.

Step Two: Qualifying

Before you make any kind of pitch, you need to do some information gathering. You need to *qualify* the customer. Your goal is to determine the following:

- Do they have a problem you can solve?
- Is that solution valuable to them?
- Is the person you are talking to capable of making a decision to do business with you?
- Do they have the money and will they spend it?
- Do they understand what you offer and its value to them?
- What is their time frame to take action?
- Do you have competition?

- Are there other services or products you offer that may appeal to them?
- Do you want to do business with them?

The answers to these questions will make the sale or tell you to stop and politely get out. Getting the information is easier than you think, but it requires one absolute: You must give them the opportunity to tell you the answers and you must listen without making any comments or judgments. Think of yourself as a wise and valued counselor who dispassionately listens before rendering a decision. Each time you ask a question, remain quiet both on the surface and on the inside as they answer. Let them answer at their own pace and resist the impulse to answer the question for them.

Listening carefully is probably the most important skill involved in selling. Your customers will always tell you everything you need to know, if you let them. Most people cannot resist the temptation to keep talking during a sales presentation. This reminds me of a great scene in the movie *Get Shorty*, where John Travolta's character is instructing Gene Hackman on how to handle a meeting with two gangsters. He carefully instructs Hackman not to say this or this but to let him handle things. Of course, as soon as the heavies sit down, Hackman's character immediately spills the beans while Travolta looks on in disgust. I've watched many amateur salespeople talk themselves into trouble in just the same way.

You begin the qualifying process by first listening to the buyers' reasons for meeting with you. Make mental notes of any answers they provide to your qualifying questions. If they open by asking you why you're there, answer with a qualifying question-statement. One example is: "I'm here to find out how I can help you with your—" (finish with a way they may use your services).

Don't get railroaded into doing your presentation on the spot. The questions you use will depend on your service or product. I suggest writing down several and using them regularly. One way to start to is to explain that your business is providing useful solutions to specific problems that the buyers are facing. If you can learn a little about the situation, you'll be able to determine whether the buyers can benefit from your help. You want to word everything from their perspective. You're telling them that by asking intelligent questions, you're seeking to save their time and to learn about their business.

Most buyers like to talk shop. Ask them if they have used a service like yours before. Ask them how it worked out. Ask them what they would do differently. Ask them the perfect world question: If this were a perfect world, how would you use my product or service and what would you like it to accomplish? Usually one good question will lead you into another. Keep the questioning brief and only ask a few. You do not want to act like this is an inquisition or interview.

Once you've asked a question, shut up. Don't ask yes–no questions. Formulate questions that require more detailed answers. Above all, listen and make notes, mental or in a small notebook. When you know what the main problem they face is and at least one advantage that excites them, you can go to the next step: Presenting your solution.

Step Three: Presentation

Presentation is the step where you explain how you can fulfill their needs and solve their problems. It's important not to start presenting until you have the information you need. Otherwise, you may waste their time and your own presenting the wrong solution or product for their needs. Your presentation must be based on what you've learned thus far.

If you have the answers to the questions we listed in the qualifying stage, you can present by addressing each question in turn and explaining briefly how you would resolve that issue. If timing is a major concern, say you have a fast response on estimates and offer to schedule around their needs. If cost is the concern, offer several options based on different budgets and any financing choices you have. If they tell you about a specific problem they face now and you have a solution or can find one, tell them what it is and how you would handle it. Everything is based on customer needs.

Presenting is an art that you can always learn more about. Each experience with each different customer will teach you things about human nature and what you do. Make it an interesting challenge and you'll do well.

PRODUCT PRESENTATIONS If you offer a physical product as a solution, your presentation is simple: Demonstrate the product in the customer's situation. For instance, if you sell a software program, explain its features in terms of how the customer's business could profit from them rather than simply listing them off. This benefits-oriented presentation is essential to selling any product. Just remember that the most important benefits are always emotional and appeal to feelings. Don't just sell the logical aspects, sell the sizzle.

PORTFOLIO PRESENTING   Presenting a service or skill is a little different, though you should always focus on benefits and an emotional connection. However, when you sell a service you do not always have a tangible product to demonstrate and show. What you do have is a track record or portfolio of what you've done in the past. The right portfolio presentation is just as effective as any product demo.

First you must have support materials prepared even if you sell an idea business like consulting. These portfolio materials must appeal to the visual, tactile, and auditory senses with pictures, graphs, examples, and stories. Start by explaining briefly what you do, from a process perspective. Rather than saying I write business books, I might say I specialize in explaining unfamiliar concepts in a way that makes them useful to my readers. In that example, I'm selling a process (communications) that I can adapt to innumerable situations. By focusing on process rather than content, I avoid being pigeonholed or tied to one past experience or job.

Set up your presentation or portfolio to demonstrate the process involved in each example. For the sake of example, I'll use the experience portfolio of a consultant. You can adapt this to nearly any service business.

THE CONSULTANT'S PORTFOLIO Jane Smith is a consultant specializing in financial planning for small business owners. While she handles several product lines including retirement funds and mutual funds, she does not feature them in her presentation. Instead, she has a portfolio of case studies based on her previous work, each example selected because it represents a different situation. Going into one sales presentation, for example, she knows from her basic research that the company is family owned and faces an unusual financial situation. This much she found out by asking two questions during her initial phone conversation.

Before leaving her office, she takes out a presentation folder and puts in three case studies of family-owned businesses, along with her brochure and business card. She has over a dozen case studies to choose from but only uses those relevant to this business. She customizes her portfolio to the sales presentation she is making today.

After qualifying her prospects, she knows which aspects of each case study will interest them and as she explains what she does, she takes each out and shows the particular problem faced and tells how she and her customer handled it. Being a financial planner requires confidentiality, so her case writeups always replace some of the specifics with generic information and alter enough of the details to make the company in question unrecognizable. She tells her clients this so they know she will respect their privacy—an important concern to these clients, as she learned while qualifying.

Jane started her portfolio while in school and made up the situations in it based on her education. This gave her a basic portfolio to use when she was getting started. Now all of her portfolio cases reflect actual situations. Each case study has charts showing how the client benefited as a result of her work as well as timelines and budget information.

The final component of Jane's presentation is to give the prospects preprinted cards with three names for them to call to check on her capabilities. She explains that these are three customers who are willing to speak frankly of their experiences and that she is not comfortable working with clients until she knows that they have done the background checking appropriate to this type of financial matter. This both builds her credibility and ensures that they will ask any competitors for similar information. This preemptive strike also eliminates any potential for competitors to bad-mouth her during their presentations. If anyone asks about other planners, she firmly states that she can't comment on the work of her colleagues because everyone works differently and every situation is different.

WRAPPING UP YOUR PRESENTATION   Once you've made your presentation, you must field questions about it. Listen and answer concisely. Go directly to the customer's concerns rather than making a general answer. If you don't have the answer, there is a magic line you must commit yourself to saying every time you don't know. That line is: *"I don't know, but I'll find out."* Once those words come out of your mouth, make a note of the question, get the answer, and get back with it as soon as possible.

No one is perfect, and there is nothing more dangerous than a person who claims to be capable of anything and to know the answer to everything. You want potential customers to see you as a resource and business partner rather than as a know-it-all or a person who simply can't admit that something is beyond his or her range of experience or interest.

Once you've made your presentation and answered any questions that come up, you're ready for the next stage, a simple yet powerful tactic called the Trial Close.

Step Four: Trial Closing

In sales parlance, the word *close* means to ask the customer to take action and close the deal with you.

Because closing involves taking a clear step and making a decision, many customers are fearful of it. Even customers strongly inclined to buy often don't volunteer to do so, and many sales presentations fail because the salesperson never asks for the business! They meet, talk, present, and then leave, feeling they've accomplished something—when the reality is that no action will result from their efforts. You must close to consummate the transaction.

The *trial close* is a test situation. It simply involves asking a closing question to flush out any hidden objections that you have not addressed yet. A closing question goes to the heart of the presentation: What you offer, how much it costs, and whether they would like to go ahead. My favorite trial closes are simple: "If we can work out [problem one] and [problem two and whatever else you know is pending], would you like to go ahead with the project?" or "If you're satisfied with my estimate and we can fit it into your schedule, would you like to go ahead with the project?"

In both examples, the answer will either be yes, in which case you set up the schedule and deal with money, or no, in which case you need to go back to qualifying and find out what objections are holding up the deal. Fortunately, because of the wording of the trial close question, your prospect will be likely to tell you what the problem is, as in: "I'm still not clear about my financing options. Do you offer a payment plan, or do

I need to come up with the money up front?" or "My wife makes those decisions; I'll have to talk to her."

In the second example, you blew it in the qualifying stage because you didn't make sure you were speaking to the right person at the beginning. Now you will have to start over and set up a time to meet with the wife (or boss or board or banker or whatever). You must try to do your sales presentation personally to this person rather than relying on the person you just spoke with to relay your message. It will lose something in the process if you leave it to your contact person to do your selling for you.

Once you've done these four steps, the actual close should happen naturally.

Step Five: Closing

Closing the deal is what selling is all about. Often sales want ads read "Closers Wanted," implying that closing is either some kind of arcane talent or that so-called closers can strong-arm buyers into signing on the dotted line. A closer is simply a person who has persisted in learning about the customer's needs, provided a solution to those needs, and asked for the business. The key words are *persistence, solutions,* and *action.* These three things are what make good salespeople—not strong-arm tactics.

The easiest close possible is a simple: "Would you like to go ahead with this now?" Once you've said these words or any other close, shut your mouth and don't say anything else, no matter what. If you are competitive, look at it this way: The first person to speak will be giving something up, even if it's to his benefit. One of the secrets of closing is to let the customer say yes.

There are many standard closes covered in books and sales training seminars. In my experience, you are best off learning one simple one and doing a good job during the sales process. The customers' answers to the closing question is a direct reflection of how well you qualified them and uncovered potential problems. It may be that they never wanted your services but couldn't say no to your face. A good qualifying sense would have uncovered that insurmountable objection and allowed you to graciously bow out. On the other hand, it is more likely that you may be the first person to sit down and really listen to their needs and address them, in which case closing is almost a formality.

Once you've made the deal verbally, you must get a written confirmation in the form of a contract, signed estimate, or a consideration such as a purchase order or deposit. Don't walk away without such a consideration. This is what binds the deal.

Step Six: Follow-Up

The best sales presentation is not complete without one critical stage, a stage that can determine the long-term prosperity of your business. That stage is the follow-up you do after the sales that results in satisfied customers, repeat business, and referrals that bring new prequalified customers to you without expensive prospecting. We'll be looking at follow-up and creating an incentive-based referral network in the next chapter.

ESTIMATES AND QUOTES

If you routinely bid on jobs and then learn if you got the work, you are still in the same sales situation even though the time frame varies. Your quote is a part of the qualifying and presenting process. Once you've prepared it and presented it, you'll learn of other objections that you must address to get the job or use to decide to decline the work.

Even when answering general requests for quotes or proposals, you must go through the sales process. Learn everything you can so you can address it in your estimate. If the request details what the customers want, cover every base thoroughly in the format they specify. Then get the names of the people handling the process and call them for more information. Do a mini qualifying interview and sales presentation over the phone. Include your brochure or fact sheets and business cards with your estimate. Call after you send it out to make sure they received it and ask if they have questions or areas you can clarify. This gives you another selling opportunity and gets your quote pulled out of the pile.

SALES TRAINING

Selling is a skill learned through hands-on experience. Neophyte salespeople will stumble and miss opportunities because they lack the experience that tells them how things are going or when they may have missed something. New salespeople also tend to focus on their own concerns, business or monetary needs, and emotional state. Sales training books, tapes, and classes or seminars are extremely valuable because they help develop skills and provide practice situations, both mental and physical.

I highly recommend that any self-employed person go out and sign up for sales training classes. In fact, a regular routine of taking a sales seminar every six months or so will refresh your skills, lend new perspective, and get you motivated to go out and become a great sales pro. In seminars you'll do hands-on role-playing with other participants, which can really change the way you do business. You'll also learn from pros and make a lot of interesting contacts. It's a lot of fun and will always improve your business ability.

Now let's get on to the next chapter and the crucial matter of after-sale follow-up. You can turn your satisfied customers into your own sales force, generating new business from others as well as repeat business from themselves.

SECTION THREE

THE
FUTURE

CHAPTER 18

FOLLOW-UP AND REFERRALS

Let's assume that your entire array of marketing tactics and strategies has worked and you've completed the sales process. You have new customers or clients—satisfied new customers, for now. They're excited about doing business with you or at least happy with the experience. They have become current customers.

It takes a lot of time and money and work to bring in new business. Even if you run a business that thrives on a steady flow of new customers, the resources required to keep that steady flow are considerable. You have to win over new customers, educate them, coddle them, and bring them up to speed. Because it costs so much to develop new business, you cannot afford to depend on new customers for your survival. You must take the next step and assure that new customers become steady customers. You should go even further and work to turn those new customers into a source of future customers through referrals and recommendations.

REGULARS AND TOURISTS

Imagine you run a diner in a busy tourist town. Each day during the busy season your signs, ads, and flyers bring in a stream of tourists who order a meal, enjoy it (you hope), and then leave. If you are fortunate, they may return several times during their stay. Even better, they may come every year and become semiregulars. And that's about the best you can hope for from these customers.

However, you have another group of customers, regulars from your town who eat every day or every week, year round. These regulars pay the bills and fill in the slow times. Many of them are dependent on the tourist business themselves as shop owners, motel operators, and workers at resorts. They are customers, friends, and, in a very real sense, business partners, because your local economy thrives on the efforts of everyone. They are also a source of endless referrals as new tourists arrive and ask for recommendations when seeking a place to eat and drink.

Your two customer groups, tourists and regulars, are no different from the customers or clients of any self-employed person. We all do jobs that last a short time and do not result in repeat business. And we all have regular customers who send us a steady stream of work. And, if we're lucky, we have a small but loyal cadre of business partners who make referrals that bring in business. These regular customers and referral sources are the key to success as a self-employed person, over the long run.

THE FOLLOW-UP PLAN

If you do not regularly follow up with your customers, you are throwing away a great part of your marketing efforts. One of the most common mistakes made by small and large businesses is ignoring or underestimating past customers as a source of business. You should have a plan for following up and ensuring that current customers remain current and a plan to turn past customers back into current ones. This follow-up plan should be automatic, with no exceptions. This is a place where using a systematic marketing tactic will really pay off.

One Week Later

Follow-up starts with a simple call after a job is complete or a sale made. The call comes one week after the completion, giving customers time to discover any problems or unexpected benefits of your work. The call simply involves you saying that you're calling to check on how they are making out with your product, whether they have any problems or questions, and to reiterate your availability to help in the future. If they have a problem, resolve it. Don't compromise or make excuses, just fix the problem. If the problem is out of your hands, put them in touch with someone who can help. Whatever you do, don't procrastinate or ignore their complaints.

This can be difficult, especially with a difficult customer, and I won't pretend that there won't be times when you just want to cut your losses and tell a customer to go elsewhere. That's your decision. However, I've found that even if the whole experience has been bad, a sincere effort on your part to make restitution or resolve the problem can turn even the most irate customer into a real believer. This is because a helpful reaction to a problem makes all of us feel better about life in general. And making your customers feel better is a very powerful way to win their support and future business.

Once a Month

After that first follow-up call, schedule at least two more over the next two months and write them into your planner. Eventually, you may be doing these calls almost daily or weekly depending on the size of your customer list. These calls can and will replace most of the cold calls you may have to make early in your marketing cycle. Instead of calling strangers, you'll be touching base with people you know and it will result in more business.

PUT THEM ON THE LIST

The final component of your follow-up regimen is to add these new customers to your mailing list and send them all the marketing and informational pieces you send out to everyone else. Because they have already done business with you, they won't view your efforts as junk mail and they'll take an interest, even if superficial, in what you're doing. It's human nature. Your mailings will remind them of your existence and give you opportunities to tell them about other products or services you offer that they may not have known about. When my brother mailed his brochure for his kitchen design business to customers who had purchased custom furniture from him in the past, he had several surprised calls from past customers who were in the process of redoing their kitchens. They knew him and his level of craftsmanship but had not realized he offered other products and services.

STICK TO YOUR LINE

Canvassing old customers to offer new services only works when the additional product lines bear a relationship to what you have offered in the past. While it would not surprise me when an electrician branched out into computer networks, I would not have an interest in that same electrician trying to sell me health supplements (something I've actually experienced). In fact, I might take offense at such a sales pitch and think about getting a new electrician who keeps his mind on his business. There should be a natural transition into new products when you offer them to old clients. When I went into the audio recording studio business, my ad agency clients were receptive to the new business because they recognized the creative link between my copywriting and audio production skills. And they had a likelihood of using both services. A lawyer pitching a recording studio would not enjoy such synergy.

Follow-up has two goals: To generate repeat business from satisfied customers and to generate referrals that bring in new customers. When the entire marketing cycle runs its course, those new customers should generate more referrals, creating a kind of automatic marketing machine to which you just need to give a little regular personal attention and communication to keep things running smoothly. To get this machine working for you, it's necessary to take an active hand in getting your customers to refer others to you.

Develop a Referral Plan

Referrals and references are the renewable power source that keeps your marketing working for you. If you don't get them or you get bad ones, all the compelling ads, publicity, and schmoozing you do will not mean much. The best marketing help you can get is a solid referral or recommendation from a respected past customer. While there will be the occasional customer who automatically thinks of you and passes your name on to others, the majority will soon forget unless you stay in their radar. A referral plan can help.

Planning to solicit referrals may seem like planning next week's weather, but it will work for several reasons. The number one reason has to do with a fundamental aspect of human nature: We feel we are better people when we can serve as a resource for others. Making recommendations is great when we can make those recommendations without reservation.

Another reason why people gladly make referrals is it makes them appear more valuable and connected. Everyone likes to be on the inside of any social group. Insiders always seem to have networks of personal connections that make it easy to keep things flowing. Being inside comes about when you consciously acquire resources and share those resources with others. The only recompense is the bank of return favors you develop, which is an asset whether or not you plan to tap into it.

The third reason people make referrals is more pragmatic: You offer them an incentive as a reward for each referral they send you. This works far better than you'd imagine with certain people. Sales managers have often found that a one-time prize like a trip or a car motivates people far more than the equivalent amount of cash. Often you can offer a small yet valued incentive to generate business.

ASK AND YE SHALL RECEIVE

So how do you get referrals? You ask for them. It's as simple as that, yet few of us would ever consider doing so. Instead, we hope that our work and the great relationships we build will cause others to automatically think of us when asked for a recommendation. Those others might recommend us, *if* they ever think of it. By asking and asking regularly, you'll keep yourself in their minds.

It's like the closing process in the last chapter. There is no use going through the entire routine of meeting, qualifying, and presenting without eventually asking outright for the sale. We can follow up methodically forever, and there will still be those who just don't think of making a referral until we come out and remind them.

This reminder can be very simple. Just say: "I'd appreciate it if you would refer anyone else you know who needs a [whatever] to me. I'll make sure they get the same high level of service you received. If you'd like, I can give you a few business cards and brochures to hang onto in case anyone asks you about this sort of thing." Always try to leave the cards and brochures. In the car business, it is standard procedure to leave a handful of business cards in the glove box of a new car when you deliver it to the customer. When you get to the cards as you go over the operations and features of the car, you explain how you'd like to see the customer use them, and give your "bird-dog speech"—that is, you outline your personal incentive plan to motivate the customer to send you more business.

INCENTIVES

In the car sales business, a *bird-dog* is a customer who points new customers to a salesperson in exchange for an incentive called a bird-dog fee. While bird-dog incentives are often cash payments (usually $50, the minimum amount found to serve as an incentive in that business), they can be simple things like dinners, small electronics items, or other gifts. Because paying cash to others for referrals may be illegal in some states, you should be careful before offering any to find out how it works in your state.

Incentives that get used up are far more valuable than durable items as referral generators, because the bird-dog will come back for more. Trips, tickets, gift certificates, and cash all have the advantage of disappearing after use, creating an interest in getting more. Also, choosing items that are luxuries that someone might not buy but will enjoy adds to the incentive. If you have a business like my recording studio, you can offer a *trade incentive*—something like one free hour of studio time for every ten hours booked by a referral.

Incentives cannot be worthless or of low value. They must represent something desirable if you want them to work as motivators. And no matter how compelling your incentive is, it won't always work for everyone. Some people (and this has little to do with income) will really go to town for you and send you business regularly; others will not have the slightest interest. Obviously, you want to aim your incentive program at the people who will really respond. Does it work? A friend refers people to a car salesman he purchased from almost 15 years ago because he loves getting those $50 bills—even though he makes a very good income. The salesman told me that my friend has resulted in as many as 30 or 40 sales over the years and that those sales were easy to close because the people had been presold as part of the referral.

TRACK YOUR INCENTIVE OFFERS

You need a system for tracking and fulfilling your incentive plan. Assuming you're following my advice and developing a database of customers on your computer or on 3 × 5 cards, simply note whether you've offered an incentive, what it was, and how often each customer has responded. The logistics of implementing an incentive plan are easy. After completing your service or delivering your product, tell customers that you appreciate referrals and that as a consideration for their recommendation, you'll throw in [whatever it is] for each customer they send you. Hand each of them a half-dozen business cards with their names written on the back for them to hand out, or simply tell them to have their referral mention their name.

Once someone refers someone to you, send out the gift immediately with a thank-you note. Even if you don't want to formally tell them about the incentive system, reward all referrals with a gift. After a few times, a good prospect will get the idea. It's a bit like Pavlov's dogs—some people will always start thinking about who else they can send to you each time you reward them. And one other thing: Don't nit-pick about paying promised referral fees. When in doubt, pay up. Those same people can do a lot of damage if you anger them by imposing too many conditions before paying.

THE BEST INCENTIVE

The best incentive you can offer people in exchange for a referral is to send them business. By returning the favor and making sure you make a steady stream of referrals to your customers' businesses and interests, you'll be starting a real referral network based on mutual benefit. You have to practice what you preach.

Making a referral to customers doesn't have to be business related. They may mention that they're considering a specific purchase and you may be able to recommend a source. This is a three-way situation. Whatever and however you make referrals, be sure that the resource you recommend is first-rate. Your credibility and reputation will be on the line.

REFERRAL FEES

Someone may ask you for a regular fee arrangement for referrals, similar to the fee arrangements common in the medical profession. Be very careful when approaching this subject as it will be subject to various tax and legal implications. I'd recommend checking with your attorney before agreeing to any regular arrangement. You may be actually contracting with someone to provide a service.

If an arrangement like this is appealing, it's probably because you're actually trying to pass your sales and marketing responsibilities on to someone else. The danger is that another person will be out there representing (or misrepresenting) your interests to potential customers. Generally, self-employed businesspeople are better off learning to sell themselves because so much of what they have to sell is personal. If you really want to pass the sales component of your business to someone else, get professional representation and expect to pay hefty commissions. There are some very effective companies that represent self-employed consultants in certain specialty areas and set them up with work in return for a cut of the fees. This can be a hybrid of self-employment and regular employment, with a mixture of benefits and pitfalls. If it works in your field, consider it—but don't let others represent your interests on a casual basis!

QUALITY GENERATES QUALITY REFERRALS

Actively pursuing referrals is really an easy process if your work is excellent, you finish things on time, and you are personable to deal with. Referrals are a vote of confidence from a customer and a show of faith in you and your abilities. When you get a referral, treat it like a very special situation even if it is a small amount of business. Respond quickly and do a superlative job. It may mean getting more business from both your customer and the new customer he or she referred.

Beware of referrals based solely on price. Pricing yourself too low is a primary reason for failure as a self-employed person because you'll eventually become chiefly known as a low-price alternative. The people who call simply because they heard you were cheap will inevitably be the ones who expect more work for less pay. They also tend to be extremely disloyal, dropping you the first time they find a cheaper alternative.

FOLLOW UP RIGHT AWAY

One of the worst things that can happen is unfortunately a very common one. People make referrals to a friend and when they ask how it went, the friend says, "I called that guy you told me about but he never returned my call [didn't show up, wasn't interested. . . .]"

Once this happens, the customer will never refer anyone to that person again and will have a bad feeling no matter how well the original job went. So don't put yourself in the position of the guy who couldn't be reached! Your actions reflect on your past customers with equal impact. Do it now and do it right.

CHAPTER 19

PROFITS AND
PROFIT CENTERS:
DUPLICATING
YOUR ABILITIES

One of the biggest challenges faced by self-employed businesspeople is the ceiling on income and future caused by being only one person. You have a limited amount of time and energy to sell in the marketplace, and this in turn limits your earning ability. Self-employment is seldom a long-term growth proposition. This leaves you few choices if you want to increase your profits and improve the kind of work you do. You can physically expand by hiring employees and becoming a small business. You can become as efficient as possible, raise your rates, and do everything you can to make the most out of your limited resources. Or you can add what I call *profit centers*. Before I look at these three choices, though, let's take a moment to define profit.

A WORD ABOUT PROFIT

I've found that many of the small business owners I work with, especially self-employed lone wolves, are confused about the idea of *profit*. All too often, they consider whatever they take home as profit. Profit is not take-home pay or salary. From an accounting point of view, any regular compensation you take out of your business is an expense, a part of your overhead the same way it would be if you paid an employee. What you have left over after expenses including overhead, salaries, cost of goods sold, and any other outgo is profit.

Profit is a measure of how well you are doing in a capitalist society as a businessperson. Profits are a major source of the capital used to grow a business. Often successful self-employed people are not seeking to grow their businesses, so any additional profits they realize go right into their pockets. Others may set aside profits for new equipment, training and education, new product development, additional marketing, and so on. Profit can also be used to pay down loan principal or pay back investors.

It is important to separate your profit from your personal salary or income for several reasons. First, you should be earning at least as much, after expenses, as you could doing the same work in the regular job market. If you're a freelance editor and your corporate counterparts are making $15 an hour, then you should be making at least that plus your overhead. Since you have to spend a certain amount on other business-related work like marketing that doesn't bring in immediate pay, you really need to make more. To figure your salary, it helps to figure out what my woodworker friends call a shop rate.

YOUR SHOP RATE

Shop rate is what you would charge by the hour to do the work you do on an hourly basis. It serves as a base rate for estimates, as a ballpark figure to throw out when you're asked for a rate, and a way to measure your rates against others in the marketplace. Here's how to figure your shop rate: Take your monthly overhead and expenses and divide by 172 (4.3 weeks × 40 hours). Add marketing and materials or inventory divided by 172, plus the average rate per hour for an employee with a similar skill set to yours. Then estimate a reasonable percentage of profit, and add that on, too.

For example (a freelance editor):

Monthly overhead	$700/172	=	4.07
Marketing and so on	$200/172	=	1.16
Average hourly wage			20.00
Profit (20%)			4.00
Total (rounded up)			$30.00

This person would have to charge about $30 an hour if she can bill customers for 40 hours per week. If she bills fewer hours on average, say 30 per week, she would need to charge more; in this example $40 per hour (40 hours times $30 = $1200 divided by 30 hours = $40). But that is not necessarily the end of the story.

Once you figure this rate, you have to look at what is common in your business and area or specialization. Perhaps our editor finds out that her competition charges $75 an hour—or $30. She will either increase her profits or decrease them to a competitive level to reach her final hourly or shop rate.

You can also figure out your shop rate on an annual basis. The formula is a little simpler:

$$\frac{\text{Annual Overhead} + \text{Desired Salary} + \text{Profit}}{\text{Actual Hours Billed}} = \text{Shop Rate}$$

Knowing your shop rate is useful from both a business and marketing viewpoint. You can estimate labor-intensive jobs by breaking down the number of hours and adding material expenses. You can easily quote small jobs on an hourly basis. You can set a minimum fee (at least two hours in most cases), and you can track just how well you're doing by tracking the hours you put into a project against the income received.

The bad news about shop rates is they may represent the theoretical ceiling of your earnings potential when you sell your time. That ceiling is the maximum number of hours you have available to sell. The only way to increase it is to cut expenses, improve efficiency, or raise your rates. Or find a way to sell your expertise without selling your time, one customer at a time. To do this, you need to identify and develop one or more profit centers associated with your business.

PROFIT CENTERS

A profit center is an action that multiplies the effects of your work so that you can sell it to many people at the same time. It can be a service, but the conventional way of thinking about profit centers is product-oriented. Let's look at an analogy to clarify this.

Suppose you could clone yourself and send all those clones out each day to do the same work you do. At the end of the day they would come home, hand you their earnings, and go to sleep until the next business day. You would sit in your office and sell your services to as many takers as you could get, and each clone you sent out would increase your income. The only upward limits to your profits would be how much work you could sell and the potential size of the market.

You can clone yourself by thinking creatively and by developing a product mentality. As a freelance marketing consultant, I can only work personally with so many clients at one time. By putting my knowledge into a book and having it marketed to the many potential clients out there like yourself, I've found a way to clone part of my skills and send those clones out to make a little money for me. Books are profit centers for me, earning money after the initial work is completed.

Profit centers can be anything easily duplicated or presented to a number of people at one time. Books, tapes, software, reports, labor-saving devices you've invented, seminars, and speeches can all be profit centers. Not only can you make money on each sale, but you get a significant marketing boost for the one-on-one work you do.

Suppose you're a therapist specializing in grief and loss. Your subject is universal and you're often asked to speak about it at organizations and conferences. While you receive a nice honorarium for these appearances, you're not really reaching your full potential. You decide to develop a seminar for the general public on coping with unexpected loss. As part of the seminar, you'll provide an informational report. You also put together a cassette tape version of the seminar for "back of the room" sales. You advertise your seminar by sending out press releases and running a few carefully placed low-key ads. You charge a basic fee for the seminar.

Your first seminar attracts 50 people who each pay $25 for the seminar and the accompanying materials. This brings in $1250, which covers your normal speaking fee and the costs of putting on a three-hour presentation. You also sell 25 tape sets at $19.95 each, for another $400 profit (after expenses). You hand out dozens of cards and several people call for your counseling services, resulting in three new clients at $75 per week each. Your average counseling relationship lasts three months, so you've added another $2700 to your annual cash flow. And you've reached and helped a large number of people, all of whom are on your mailing list for additional seminars, future books, counseling referrals, and similar opportunities.

The seminar and tapes are both profit centers. Eventually, you (our therapist) get asked to present your materials to larger groups. You make a publishing deal to have a publisher market the tapes and books to a broader audience. The profit centers have increased your realm of influence, your reputation, and your profits. You spend about 20 hours per month on them—and your average hourly rate for that activity is about $200 per hour when you add up royalties, sales, and fees over a year.

IDENTIFYING YOUR PROFIT CENTERS

Almost every self-employed person has potential profit centers. Hairdressers sell hair care products. Musicians sell tapes and CDs. Electricians may handle a line of lighting fixtures. Writers resell articles to secondary markets. Interior designers sell everything imaginable for an interior, marking everything up by a significant amount. Graphic designers make a mark-up on printing jobs. You have to think creatively about the things you sell and look for parts of that package that can be reproduced or presented to many people at once.

Mark-Ups

A common profit center for many self-employed people comes from marking up the cost of materials and services you buy as part of a job. If you don't do this, you should—you're spending time and money to find and maintain these resources. If you're a painter buying paint for a job and get a commercial discount for it, you should mark the paint up to retail—and add in the time you spent at the paint store. Otherwise, you're giving away your time. Mark-ups don't have to be onerous. Be reasonable with them and take care to add enough but not too much. If a client finds out you're marking an item up several hundred percent—you'll lose a customer.

Inventions and Licenses

As an expert in your field, you've probably had an idea at one time or another that you thought had potential as an invention or a licensable concept. An invention is a new and unique way of doing something. *Licensing* is a way of profiting from intellectual property by licensing it to others for manufacture or reproduction and marketing. Things like royalty payments based on a percentage of sales or a per-unit amount are licensing arrangements.

Taking an idea beyond the light bulb stage is challenging. It requires learning a whole new set of skills and acquiring knowledge in areas like intellectual property law, fundraising, marketing, and manufacturing. You must produce a working prototype, a name, and a marketing angle. This all requires cash and time. You must do considerable research to determine if a market exists and if that market will be profitable.

You must also protect and defend your idea. The written word is automatically protected under U.S. copyright law. However, copyright only protects that actual wording and does not protect you from anyone rewriting and presenting your ideas in a slightly different format. The best way to protect a written idea is to be first in the market, choose a compelling title, and market your idea aggressively.

Physical inventions are protected to some degree by *patents* issued by the government, which give you exclusive legal protection. However, patents are not easy to get. They often cost a lot of money, and they may not offer sufficient protection from copycats who have similar but slightly different inventions. Again, you must build as many layers of protection as possible, including unique names, taglines, logos or trademarks, packaging, and all of the many marketing tools available that differentiate McDonald's from Burger King and the world's other fast food outlets. A patent attorney is essential—consult one at the beginning of any invention or idea development process. There are also numerous books available on the subject. Stay away from companies that promise to promote your invention for a steep fee. They are almost always frauds aimed at hapless wishful thinkers.

Trademarks

If you have a unique, interesting, or compelling name or logo, you should consider applying for trademark status. A registered trademark protects you from any other company's using similar names or images. Unlike copyright, a solid trademark offers considerable legal protection and can become a very valuable asset. Trademarks can be business or product names, logos, slogans, your name, characters, and other representations unique to your business. Again, you need an experienced intellectual property lawyer to search and register a trademark for you.

Once you have a trademark, you may find that it has value to others. Amazingly enough, our society now pays good money for items emblazoned with advertising and logos of various companies. We have whole stores full of Nike clothing, Warner Brothers gifts, and other licensed apparel and products. You don't have to be a giant business like these to cash in on your trademark. If you have a business sufficiently unique, hip, or well located, you may be able to sell products featuring your logo—T-shirts, bumper stickers, hats, and so on.

Franchises

Another way to profit is to license your trademark along with your business concept to others in different geographic areas through a franchising setup. While franchising seems beyond the means of a self-employed person, companies like Mrs. Field's Cookies started out as one-person operations. Franchising involves system-atizing your entire business so that it becomes a turnkey operation that anyone can run after some standardized training and then adding a marketing package with a recognizable and proven name and image to create a complete package you can sell over and over. It's complex but possible.

Employing Others

Employees are a form of profit center. The decision to hire and train an employee is very similar to attempting to clone part of your skills so that you can spread out the work and serve more customers. Because an employee is a version of you, it's vital to choose the right person—an increasingly difficult challenge. An employee must be trainable, reliable, trustworthy, and willing to do things your way. If you hire someone with his or her own way of doing things, you're taking on a partner rather than an employee no matter who the boss is now. Eventually, differences will arise and you'll either relinquish part of your authority and control or terminate the relationship.

From a marketing perspective, the only way to view an employee is as a profit center. You hire and train them and mark up their work. They make $10 and you make $15, clearing a good profit on their work. If this is not the case, you're employing a person for reasons other than profit. Maybe you want company, are merely supplying a friend with a job, or don't want to work as much yourself. These are legitimate reasons—but have little to do with successful marketing as they don't build your business or profits.

DO YOU WANT PROFIT CENTERS?

Profit centers and product development are a fascinating aspect of running a business for some people. It's not unusual for self-employed people to discover that they are more interested in concept and marketing than actually doing the work. This entrepreneurial mindset is ideal for making profit centers or products the central part of your business and letting others do the day-to-day work. For others, the freedom they find in just doing what they do well outweighs the complexity of trying to build a bigger business. It is your choice, and neither is the wrong one. I hope you'll consider the possibility of doing a little of each. Developing even a few small profit centers can mean always having the money to pay bills or sock away something for the future. From a marketing viewpoint, these value-added products and services also build your awareness level with all your customers, old and new.

CHAPTER 20

COMPETITION
AND PRICING

You may have noticed that I have not spent a lot
of time on the subject of competition, particularly
when it comes to effectively marketing against it. After
all, when you win business, someone else loses, right?
The language of marketing does resemble the language
of warfare with its strategies and tactics. You hear about
big companies battling for market share the way coun-
tries at war seek to take each other over. And what
about cutthroat pricing and other similar terms that
make business sound like a battlefield?

I don't subscribe to the marketing-as-warfare
analogy, particularly with very small businesses. To be
honest, I don't really think about competition either, at
least not in the conventional confrontational sense. To

put it simply, if you do an exceptional job at market prices and offer special expertise and a personal and appealing approach, you probably don't have much competition. You may have companions in the same business as you and they may occasionally get work that you bid on, but they are seldom your enemies. In fact, they may be potential allies, especially when you're talking about other self-employed people.

ONE OF A KIND

The reason for my cavalier attitude about competition is the basic nature of the self-employed businessperson: You are almost always one of a kind, a unique combination of skills, experience, and personality. This unique combination is what your customers want when they come to you for your products or services. If they continue to do business with you, a big part of the reason will be the personal chemistry between you and your customers. And if they buy solely based on price or flavor-of-the-month thinking, they are unlikely to remain loyal for long.

Your direct competition is another person like you in some ways, who may or may not be self-employed. If he is a part of a big company, his relationship with your potential customers still comes down to personal relationships. I occasionally hire a plumber for various projects. The company I do business with is quite large, with a dozen or so crews on the road. However, I have always dealt with the same employee there, and he is the principal reason I deal with them rather than their competition. In fact if this person were to leave and go elsewhere, I'd probably want to continue to work with him rather than stay with his previous employer.

The reason this is important is that many of us tend to wonder when we hear about competition. Did they get the job and why? Will they charge less? How can I compete with a big company and its deep pockets, numerous employees, and other advantages? Is this going to hurt my livelihood? These are important concerns. Fortunately, you have powerful resources to address and alleviate them.

First of all, the majority of your competition will do little or no effective marketing. As absurd as it seems, look around. Do a little research on them. Read their ads, if any; call and ask for information; send a friend to meet them or shop their place of business; and ask others what they have heard. You'll find out a lot. If everything they are doing is impressive, then you must at least match their efforts. If you hear or learn about weaknesses, make them your strengths.

My guess is you'll find that they are much like yourself. After reading a book like this one, the first thing you've probably learned is how little you are doing to promote yourself. They are no different except they may not have actually started to take action to change the situation. You have. You're sitting here working on your marketing.

USES OF COMPETITORS

This illustrates one very valuable use of competition. It gives you something to compare yourself to. How good is their work and why? If they are cheaper but appear to prosper, what are they doing more efficiently? Even more important, are they getting a higher rate? (More about rates and pricing later in this chapter).

Competitors also spur you on. They are a great source of motivation. If someone is reaching out to eat your lunch, you better grab faster or you'll go hungry. This kind of motivation is reactive: You take action in reaction to another event. While it usually helps to be first, if you're not, then "go to school" on your competition. (A golfer goes to school on another golfer when they both have a similar putt and one goes first, giving the other a learning opportunity.) If you are a financial planner and one of your competitors is offering a seminar, attend the seminar and see how it goes. Check out their tactics and adapt what works. In marketing, imitating success is a proven technique.

Your competitors offer another kind of potential resource: They may be a source of business. This is common when you share a similar skill like copywriting but have different specialties. You do a lot of medical writing, I handle entertainment. If a pharmaceutical firm approaches me for an annual report, I may refer them to you, while you'd send me a film company. It may sound idealistic, but it happens all the time in many businesses. Consider calling your competition and meeting to see if you can be referral partners.

If a direct call is too much, this is a good reason to network with your peers by joining associations or attending events like shows and conferences. Peer networking is designed to generate expert referrals or professional courtesy referrals. Writing articles and getting other forms of publicity may also help connect you with your competition in a positive way.

You may also find yourself in an overflow situation. You've read this book, done everything I suggest, and now you're swamped. Your competitors may now start looking like potential business partners. Call them and suggest a business relationship. Tell them the price you're willing to pay, the circumstances, and the discount you'll pocket for delivering the work. If someone offers you a $1,000 job you're too busy to take, you may be able to handle the customer end and let someone else do the work for less money, picking up your profit from the difference.

This should work both ways; if it doesn't, find another partner. You also must beware of dealing with partners whose work is an unknown or who are untrustworthy. You can get burned badly by incompetence or having your customers stolen out from under you. It's a risk.

Shop Talk

Your competitors are also the ones who know the most about your business—because it's their business as well. Because of this, you should think of them as potentially valuable information sources. No matter that you know you lost a bid to someone you just met at a show. Ask them how it went. Let them know you bid and talk a little shop. It's amazing what you can pick up, hearing everything from gossip to who's seeking what resources. Don't ignore gossip; often you'll find out about personnel changes, promotions, new interest areas for your customers, and other useful things.

Shop talk covers everything from technical stuff to airing complaints about past work or customers. You may learn to not offer credit to a customer from a competitor who learned the hard way. You may also hear that a large company is expanding or using a lot of contractors or outside help. This scuttlebutt is the lubricant that keeps relationships going in many businesses. Keep an ear out—beneath the veneer of small talk and grousing, you'll hear a lot of deals in progress and find out about a lot of opportunities. If you participate, you might learn something. If you don't, you definitely won't.

Badmouthing and Sour Grapes

One last note about competition: Don't ever badmouth the other guy. It will come back to haunt you in ways you cannot predict. Remember how I compared networking within a specialized industry to living in a small town? Like a small town where everybody knows everything, your badmouthing will get back to someone you don't want it to.

The usual effect of hearing someone speak poorly of a fellow businessperson is to think that it smells slightly of sour grapes. Comparing yourself favorably to someone else also has this taint. Instead, praise what is different in both of you. Say: "I've always admired the way she handles such and such. I've always been a little stronger in the other end of the business." Stay positive and hand out professional courtesy rather than scorn.

BIDS, QUOTES, AND ESTIMATES

Pricing is where we typically get wrapped up in worrying about the competition. It's very common for potential customers to ask a self-employed person for quotes, bids, or estimates. When you price work, consider it first from what you must earn to justify taking the job. This doesn't always include only monetary issues; it also involves time, degree of stress involved, potential for future long-term relationships, and so on. However, you must always charge at least your minimum price based on your shop rate as calculated in the last chapter.

Professionals do not work for free. It contradicts the entire meaning of being professional and it lowers the perceived value of your work down to the cheapest price you charge. Once you've worked on the cheap for a customer, they will always expect the same. Many of my friends and family are self-employed or own businesses, and we have an unwritten rule that you do not ask friends to do something they earn a living at for free. In other words, I don't ask my painter friend to stop by and help me paint my house on a Saturday afternoon without paying him. If he offers, I weigh the situation and usually try to pay something.

It is no different when someone asks you to work cheaply or for free with a vague promise of future work. Don't do it. In these situations, these people are inevitably moving from vendor to vendor asking until some desperate character takes them up on it. Then, if they ever have money, will they turn to that desperate guy? Of course not; they want a professional. In our world, commanding and receiving a decent payment for services is what earns respect, trust, and future business.

Fear of Being Too High

A common mistake many of us make, particularly when starting out, is to price our work too low at the last minute because of various fears and misconceptions. These include fear of offending or scaring away customers, fear of making people mad, fear of losing work we really need, and other delusions. I've found that if you do good work, you should suffer from a different kind of fear: Fear of charging too little.

When I quote a job, I break down my time and expenses, add profit, and look at the final number. I consider the client and what I know about his resources from my qualifying questions. I also consider how busy I am and how interesting the work is. Then I adjust the price. If I'm always adjusting up, then my basic rate is too low; if I always end up high, then I must face reality and lower my prices.

While it depends on your business, you are better off from a marketing point of view being a little high than being the low bidder. For one thing, it is common practice in a bidding situation for a customer to discard both low and high bids. Second, you set a precedent that's hard to change. Third, you'll attract a more financially sound customer who is willing to pay well for value received.

Don't Drain the Well

If you know the customer's budget for a project or have some idea of their cash flow, don't automatically price your work to use up their money. Graphic designers are particularly guilty of this. I've seen many instances where I came in as a marketing consultant to a small business owner who proudly showed me a beautiful brochure and a half-dozen full-page ads prepared by a local designer. Unfortunately, they weren't sending out those brochures or running those ads because the designer had spent the entire marketing budget on the design end of the package, leaving nothing to build up cash flow with. When you price a job, price it to help your customers succeed. If they can't meet your rate, ask them to meet with you to figure out a way to gradually implement your help.

Go Where the Money Is

As a final note on pricing, I have a personal rule I'd like to pass on that took me a while to figure out. Once I learned it, I increased my income by about 100 percent, which surely qualifies it as good marketing advice. Simply put, go where the money is. In other words, don't spend a lot of energy marketing yourself to small operators. People who think small don't like paying for anything even if the service or product they're buying will make them money. They also don't like delegating work to anyone else, one of the reasons they stay small.

Instead, aim your efforts at those who can and will pay the price you feel is fair for your work. If you sell to businesses, concentrate your efforts on successful businesses with a track record of using self-employed people. If you sell to individuals, look for prosperous, well-educated people who understand business. This is not elitist, it is common sense; yet I know many self-employed people who seem to think that it is their mission to educate people about what is good for them while taking whatever money they have. You can skip this labor-intensive and unrewarding task by going to the customers who already understand the value of what you offer.

THE RIGHT PRICE

Pricing your work right and knowing your competition are marketing skills that take time to acquire. Like all skills, you pick them up through trial and error. I've often found that people starting out as self-employed business owners are looking for a price list that will tell them what to charge. While some business areas may have such lists, they are guidelines at best. There is only one rule of pricing in a free market society: The right price is the one that someone is willing to pay.

Another common misconception when starting out is to fear and mistrust your competition. It is similar to the inventor who steps into the patent attorney's office, looking nervously over his shoulder. When the attorney asks how he can help, the guy says he has invented a device that will change the world. However, he is unable to divulge anything about it and is so paranoid that he is never able to share his discovery with anyone else. In most cases, your competitors are more likely to be sympathetic allies than cutthroat enemies. Even if they are not sympathetic, they are seldom as interested in what you do as what they are doing, a bit of human nature that you can turn to your advantage by keeping a friendly but observant eye and ear open.

CHAPTER 21

TIME AND
THE FUTURE

Marketing yourself is a long-term project. Every action you take now will have repercussions for years to come, as you build awareness, develop relationships with customers, and evolve your business. The marketing you're doing today may not generate business for weeks or months, but it will eventually reach customers—often in ways that no one could foresee. That's why it's vital to consider the future as you plan and implement your marketing.

For many self-employed people, work is a roller coaster. One month you're swamped, the next you're idle. Some enjoy this unpredictable schedule, but others find it extremely frustrating never knowing how busy they'll be or whether they'll have enough cash flow to pay the bills. The only way out of this cycle is to continuously market yourself, especially when you're busy.

It is tempting to let your marketing efforts slow when things get hectic. You're doing well and the need for new business doesn't seem as pressing as it did when you were idle. Plus you're busy and stretched for time just to stay on schedule. It can be hard to imagine even having any time for marketing, much less interrupting every day to keep at it. Yet it is these periods when you stop promoting yourself that eventually lead to the next lull. No marketing today, no business tomorrow.

CLOCKWORK MARKETING

The only way to keep your marketing on track when you're busy is to have a systematic approach. Once you've created a plan, made a schedule, and set aside resources to implement that plan, you should be able to go on autopilot when you're busy, dedicating a few minutes every day to keep the marketing machine running smoothly. It's like a clockwork toy: Your planning winds it up and it keeps ticking along. All you have to do is spend a little time each day oiling the gears and winding the spring.

When you're busy, limit your marketing to one or two simple actions each day and do them habitually. Perhaps they may involve finding the name and address of one new potential customer and dropping a brochure and personalized sales letter in the mail each morning followed by one phone call to an earlier recipient of the same package. A few minutes at the computer and five minutes on the phone are all it takes.

Another approach is to dedicate time not spent working to a weekly marketing activity. Lunch is a time period that can combine a personal meeting with eating and getting away from work. Make one lunch appointment per week with a client or customer. Block out a specific amount of time and avoid stretching it out. Discuss business informally and ask your clients how their business is going. Any casual business-related subjects are fine, including shop talk, industry gossip, or upcoming projects. The idea is not to make a sale on the spot but to keep in touch and gather information.

THE ADVANTAGES OF MARKETING WHEN YOU'RE BUSY

These incremental efforts eventually add up and keep you in the habit of marketing yourself constantly regardless of how frantic your lifestyle has become. When you're busy, you have several significant marketing advantages. First, you are in *work mode,* a state of mind where you stay focused and get down to business quickly. This impresses and motivates others and may inspire them to take advantage of your in-gear approach.

Second, when you're busy you have the ability to say no to marginal or low-priced projects. When you're busy, it is only worth your while to spend your valuable time on the most interesting, profitable projects. You may quote higher prices, ask for more resources, or bid only on the parts of a job that interest you. In one of the great paradoxes of self-employment, this approach often makes you more desirable in the eyes of your customers. We've all heard someone say they want to work with so-and-so if they get the opportunity. They're willing to wait, up to a point, for the busy resource that appears to really be in demand.

Charging more often attracts better customers, particularly when you work with larger companies—they tend to view the higher-priced supplier as being more stable and reliable. You have the luxury of trying this approach when you're busy. The third advantage of being busy is that you have more resources at hand. Usually you have extra money to spend on marketing, and this may be the time to get started on a new brochure or seminar to generate new business or introduce a new product or service.

MARKETING IN SLOW PERIODS

When things are slow, you may not have the monetary resources you do when cash flow is steady but you do have another priceless commodity: Time. The problem is we often get out of work mode when there's no specific deadline ahead to motivate and activate us. It's not uncommon for business owners in a slump to procrastinate about activities like marketing that don't immediately result in paying work. This is a slippery slope, because being idle and failing to promote yourself will snowball and you may go out of business.

The key is time. You've got it and it's not costing you anything. If you don't use it, it will disappear forever. Time is the great equalizer in life and in business. The smallest shopkeeper and the busiest millionaire have exactly the same number of hours in the day. It's how they use them that makes the difference. We've all seen books on time management, and it is such a popular subject for seminars and training that it has almost become a cliché—but it is an essential skill, especially when it comes to marketing.

TIME MANAGEMENT

The rewards of effective time management are obvious when you're super-busy: You squeeze out a few more minutes to get everything done. But it's when you've got time to spare that time management can have its least expected effect. Suddenly finding yourself off the treadmill after a busy period and unsure where work will come from can be disorienting and disheartening. You make the shift from a full schedule and regular doses of the satisfaction that comes from getting results to an empty day followed by more empty days. It's actually easier to schedule your time when you've got a lot of things to accomplish than it is when you're not sure what to do.

This is where the power of effective time management comes in. We've all thought longingly of what we'd do if we only had the time, especially when we're busy. Most daily planners available today have sections dedicated to longer-range goals and journal entries. Even when you're busy, it's a good idea to jot down these "if only" activities. Sometimes when you're in the thick of things you're more receptive to the potential of what you do than when you're out of the loop. Keep notes on potential projects as they come to you, no matter how far-fetched. They'll be useful when things slow.

Take the time each morning during slow periods to schedule your entire day. Even if your schedule says "11:00–11:30, Walk the dog. 11:30–12:00, Have coffee and call your sister," you'll be getting back into work mode. As you schedule, schedule in the same incremental marketing actions we discussed earlier, that is, one call and one mailing daily. These should be sacrosanct activities done so automatically they become akin to brushing your teeth or having coffee each morning. Various performance studies have shown that, on average, if you perform the same action daily for 21 days it becomes a habit. Make this minimal marketing activity a habit.

PROJECT MARKETING

So what else do you schedule? I recommend that you develop a simple marketing project that requires little money but does require a concentrated effort and dedicated amount of time. This project should last no longer than a week and should achieve some kind of measurable results so that it won't interfere with upcoming work. The results are important because they get you back into that work-reward cycle that you thrive on in busy periods. Once you've settled on a project, finish it even if it means telling potential customers that you won't be available until next week. It's seldom that this will cause any problems.

What is a *marketing project?* It's an action that is concentrated, has specific goals and a measurable result, and can be accomplished with the resources at hand. A good example is researching and identifying a new customer group or market segment. Let's look at an example.

JEAN'S ESPRESSO CART

Jean runs an espresso coffee cart in the first-floor atrium of a busy office building. Her day starts early; she has a very busy period from 6:30 to 9:00 and then another during the coffee break around 11:00. She does a steady business through lunch and then spends several hours in the afternoon standing around waiting to fill the occasional order. She is busy enough in the winter. Now, in

(continues)

the summer months, her day is basically over around 11 A.M. She's got some time and she wants to figure out how to increase business and stay busy all day.

Jean decides that she will spend her slow afternoons for a week hunting for a source of steady customers and will then consider moving her cart there or purchasing another and hiring a helper to run it. She starts with nothing more than a notepad and a pen and begins listing all the public spaces in her area, noting down who frequents them and when they are likely to be busy. Because the weather in her area is changeable, she eliminates outdoor areas. She also eliminates other office buildings like the one she is in now because their schedules are similar. Eventually she is down to the area shopping malls, hotel lobbies, conference centers, museums and galleries, colleges, and sporting facilities—both arenas and health clubs. It takes her two afternoons to create her list, and she enlists her steadiest customers in her project, generating ideas she hadn't considered such as libraries and corporate training centers.

Jean closes her cart down at 3 and still has two hours in her working day. When she is busy in the winter months, she spends this time winding down and cleaning and restocking her cart. In the summer, she has these actions done by noon and is ready to do almost anything by the time 3 P.M. rolls around. After her list is complete, she decides to visit each site on the list and check for traffic, competition, and likely locations for a cart. She'll also try to get a contact name for each of the best candidates.

She gets a map of the area and plans to visit two to three sites each day. After visiting seven locations, she finds two that have a steady stream of people and no competing carts or coffee shops. They are both, surprisingly, college student unions. She hadn't considered that most colleges either offer summer classes or run quarterly programs through the summer now. She also has the names of their building managers.

She calls them both and tells them about her business and inquires about locating a cart in their facility. One nibbles at the idea and agrees to a meeting for the next week.

Jean's project has yielded a potential expansion opportunity for her small business with very little use of resources other than time. In the next few weeks, she takes advantage of her summer slow period to plan a change, weigh opportunities, decide whether to expand or move her operation, and look into financing options. By the time the summer is winding down, she has a new

(continues)

location frequented by students clamoring for lattés and espressos to keep them going through their classes. She has added a few tables, and there is a social scene around her cart that continues until 10 at night seven days a week, necessitating the hiring and training of helpers. Once she learns to handle employees, Jean begins to think about licensing her concept to others on college campuses nationwide, another potential marketing project.

Not all projects will succeed like Jean's. She could easily have decided that taking on employees and longer hours was not for her, an equally valuable discovery. In that case, her project would still have yielded results without a big expense in time or money. Some other marketing projects might include:

- New product development
- Learning a new skill
- Developing a seminar
- Writing a book proposal
- Calling 50 new customers
- Surveying your past customers to discover why they are not doing business with you

- Taking a business class
- Writing a marketing plan
- Working for someone else
- Running a week's worth of classified ads in a daily paper and tallying the results
- Finding new sources for supplies and products
- Computerizing your marketing
- Creating a customer database
- Observing your competition at work

Choose a project for your next slow period and start planning it now. Then when the schedule empties out, you'll find that you've still got plenty to do. In fact, you'll be just as busy doing something for yourself and your future.

LONG-TERM GOALS

For time management techniques to be really effective, they need to be long term. When you look far ahead and make longer-range plans for your work and your life, you can accomplish almost anything. It's when you're so busy that you can barely imagine making it through the next week that time seems to stand still. If life seems to be passing you by while you toil away on the same old regimen, it is a clear sign that you need longer-range goals.

In business, it takes time to make changes. You have to plan, research, accumulate resources, and take step after step toward your goal. And all of this must take place while you're out making a living. As self-employed people, we don't have teams of long-term planners creating interesting new situations for us. Only our own actions will result in beneficial changes in what we do.

Surprisingly, it often does not take a big effort to change the nature of your work if you use time to spread out the work. A commercial photographer who decides to get into digital imaging has two choices. He can put everything aside, dive in and purchase all the computing power necessary (along with the complex software the work requires), and try to learn how to use it. He'll spend a lot of money and may not be skilled enough to get immediate work. By making proficiency in this medium a two-year goal, the whole process becomes much clearer. He can buy a reasonably good computer and take lessons to learn the basics of the software. When things are slow, he can practice on his own photos and eventually develop a speculative portfolio. When he develops proficiency, he can use some of those practice pieces as marketing tools, perhaps doing a series of intense postcards with a wild image on one side and a marketing message on the other. Sent to his regular clients and to lists of new prospects (another gradual project), the cards will gradually ease him into his new venture. Finally, when the market justifies it, he can upgrade to a state-of-the-art imaging work station and hang out his new shingle full time.

Every self-employed person should have some longer-term project in mind. This is work you do for yourself, to enhance your own work life and generate more interesting projects. This is not just a luxury. Change occurs so rapidly these days that you can find yourself out of business, replaced by technology or deserted by a disappearing market. By looking ahead and trying to anticipate future directions, you'll change with the times and prosper.

FLOW STATES

Time is not a static commodity. An hour spent in a tedious task can seem many times longer than one spent on something you find fascinating. As the clock ticks, each minute is the same—but as we perceive them they are very different. Psychologists and physicists have been investigating the reason for this for a long time; recent research focuses on what are sometimes called *flow states.*

Flow states are periods of intense focus when we experience the sensation of being completely immersed in life. Moments can take on intense degrees of clarity and we can function at a higher level, accomplishing exceptional creative and athletic achievements. Once considered the exclusive territory of world-class athletes and geniuses, it is now apparent that we all experience these flow states at various times in our lives.

The value of flow states in the context of marketing and self-employment lies in the way they can
enhance creative thinking and problem solving. Often,
when you are deeply immersed in some challenging aspect of your work, you tap into an almost instantaneous
source of creativity. It can happen when you're in the
middle of a sale, working on developing new products,
or working with others in a collaborative project. Keep
your mind open to suggestions or ideas that surface
when you're working at full capacity. They may be
messages from your own subconscious offering you
new ways to prosper in the future.

A FINAL NOTE

We've covered a lot of territory in *Marketing for the Self-
Employed*. The ideas can be overwhelming at first. That's
why I ended with a little discussion of something as esoteric as flow states. The real value of a book like this
lies in its ability to get you thinking. If you take only a
few of the marketing actions here and apply them frequently and consistently, you'll be way ahead of your
competition. The fact is that many self-employed people
do no conscious marketing. They move along, talking
about their work (often from their own narrow
perspective), occasionally handing out business cards,
and making excuses for not consciously working on
promoting their business. They've closed their minds to
the potential.

As you think about things that strike you while reading this book, I hope you've kept your mind open. Often changes we have never considered making can turn our work world around. I have a friend who is a talented interior designer. For her first three years in business, she used her name followed by "Interior Design" as her business name. This is a standard approach in the design world. However, she has an Eastern European name that is virtually impossible to pronounce just by reading it unless you're of the same background. She resisted changing her business name, but eventually I convinced her to try another approach. The effect of a simple name change was amazing. The number of calls, referrals, and responses to her marketing doubled almost overnight because people could call without the embarrassment of mispronouncing her name.

Whether you change your name, take on a new skill, try actively selling rather than passively waiting, or simply upgrade your business cards for a fresh look, you've taken action. Taking any action to market yourself is a step forward and will generate results.

Small changes can make a big difference. Incremental marketing actions taken daily add up over time. A series of small decisions is much easier to get through than making one big decision. Doing a better job is vital. And telling the world how you can solve the problems you're skilled at solving is the essence of successful marketing. Good luck is mostly good planning and doing something useful—so good luck to you!

SAMPLE
MARKETING PLAN

This sample marketing plan can serve as a general guide and example for your own plan. It draws on the research and planning processes covered in Section One and employs some of the marketing tactics covered in Section Two. I've kept it brief while noting many optional tactics to give the business owner choices based on changing priorities and available time and resources.

Because self-employment encompasses a wide range of businesses, skills, and product offerings, this plan may at first glance seem to have little relevance to your own work. However, the process involved in marketing yourself is similar, and the basics are the same for almost every business. Besides, this sample is mainly to encourage you to write a simple plan for yourself—if you don't like it, fix it! Even the largest businesses seldom need a complex marketing plan; yours should be as simple as you can make it.

The plan is for a one-person consulting business specializing in helping other businesses develop a presence on the Internet. The business involves designing systems and content for business Web pages and helping those businesses increase awareness of their Internet services. While our imaginary company, CyberPlace, is a one-person business, the plan is written as though for a larger company because the owner may wish to expand in the future. His market research has also shown that his target clients are more likely to respond to a company than an individual.

A plan like this requires a businesslike tone because the owner may wish to include it in an overall business plan created to generate financial investment or a bank loan. An effective and compelling marketing plan is one of the first things that investors and loan officers consider, because they know that a business plan that does not show marketing savvy is likely to fail. If you include your plan in a larger business plan, attach supporting documents including copies of promotional pieces like brochures and sales letters, your logo, any good press you've received, and letters from potential clients indicating their willingness to use you for future or ongoing projects. These documents support both your marketing plan and your projections regarding financial results.

Your plan may be much simpler or much more complex based on your business. Start brief and simple and you'll be far more likely to reap the benefits of your marketing. Overly ambitious efforts may prove overwhelming and have the effect of turning avid marketers into nonmarketers. Put your plan in writing and share it with anyone helping with your marketing, including designers, account executives, and other marketing pros. If they are aware of your overall objectives, they will be able to help you achieve them.

CYBERPLACE ASSOCIATES— MARKETING PLAN FOR 199X

This plan defines our marketing objectives and activities for the next year. It consists of product information, targeted market sectors, strategy, and a schedule and budget. Finally, it suggests several areas for future growth or change.

Business Description
CyberPlace Associates is a consulting firm specializing in helping growing companies develop a

(continues)

presence on the Internet. Our specialty is creating and designing Internet sites that are extremely efficient and compelling, with entertaining and informative content that users can download easily without long waiting periods. We take pride in clearly educating and training our clients so they can upgrade and maintain their sites themselves with little effort and limited additional expense.

Products and Services

Our primary product is our expertise and experience at demystifying the cyber marketplace. We offer our clients an easy path to entering the Internet and establishing a presence that can benefit their business in measurable ways. The primary features of our products are ease of use by both clients and the Internet community; a hip, user-friendly design ethic; and flexibility to change as the technology changes.

The benefits to our clients of doing business with us are significant savings in time and money because of our emphasis on training and simple interface design, measurability of responses to their Internet presence, and a wide-open upgrade path, keeping them up to date and limiting hardware obsolescence.

Target Markets

Because we provide personal, on-site service and training, our primary target market is the geographic area bordering our city. However, as demand changes, we will travel to clients in any part of the world—we recognize that the Internet knows no borders. Our primary customers are information technology companies with sales in the $1–$25 million range. These companies have customer bases that are familiar with online use and are computer savvy, making an Internet presence a logical and profitable marketing need.

We will target our marketing at the presidents and CEOs of these companies using a top-down approach because in companies at this level top executives tend to be very hands-on and heavily involved in the decision-making process. Our market research shows that the number of potential clients in our area numbers approximately 50 and the bulk of our marketing will target these 50 executives and their companies.

Strategy

The business community in our area is relatively insular, with most company owners and executives at least familiar with their peers. To reach

(continues)

this tight-knit community, our marketing will focus on developing personal relationships with client company executives, providing effective and measurable results, and generating referrals from those executives.

We will accomplish this by taking a series of actions designed to promote our name and reputation and by engaging in personal marketing. These actions will include regular publicity and participation in community business activities, among other tactics.

Tactics

Our company name is a significant asset, and we will protect and promote it as such. We will register "CyberPlace, Your Business Portal to the Internet" as a trademark, along with a professionally designed, compelling, and cutting-edge logo that accurately reflects our business style.

We will develop an up-to-date and accurate list of names and contact information by making calls to each potential client company and requesting the information. This list, which we will maintain as a database, will be the basis of all of our marketing efforts. We will also develop a media list including local business media and trade media that our potential clients are likely to read.

All list members will receive a minimum of six direct mail pieces per year. These will consist of a capabilities brochure, a personal letter, copies of recent publicity articles, invitations to seminars, a case study report on a successful project, and other relevant information.

Our principal will call all list members personally to introduce our service and set up meetings to present our sales presentation. Our goal is to give one sales presentation per week until we are too busy, and then scale back to one or two per month.

We have a Web site that serves as an ongoing demonstration portfolio of our work and contains information, demonstrations, and easy-to-use direct e-mail response questionnaires. To demonstrate our Web site to non-Internet clients, we bring a laptop computer to their office, dial up, and walk them through the process of logging on and using a browser to reach our site.

We will use publicity on a regular basis to promote our business, including articles about Internet marketing in the business media, press releases for all new developments, and availability for interviews on any Internet subjects. As support for our publicity we will run small, professionally written and designed ads in the

(continues)

same publications where we receive publicity. These ads will run year round and will constitute a regular business expense.

We will run a Yellow Pages ad under Internet Services. All marketing and Web sites will feature Internet addresses and links to our Web pages.

Schedule

Daily: Respond to requests for information. Two cold calls to potential clients.

Weekly: One sales presentation, one lunch meeting, attend one association meeting or function. Run weekly ad in *Metro Business Weekly*. Hand out ten business cards.

Monthly: Speak on Internet subjects at meetings. Run one ad in *City Business Magazine*. Send out press release and call all media contacts for follow-up.

Bimonthly: Mail all client and media contacts one direct mail piece.

Semiannually: Offer Internet Business Seminar

Annually: Revise Marketing Plan.

Budget

Weekly: Advertising $35, postage $10, miscellaneous including lunches $30; total: $75.

Monthly: Advertising $50, Other $50, Total: $100.

Bimonthly: Direct Mail: $200.

Semiannual: Seminar: $500.

Annual Totals: Weekly Expense × 52 = $3,900.

Monthly × 12 = $1,200.

Bimonthly × 6 = $1,200.

Semiannual × 2 = $1,000.

Annual Total = $7,300.

Brochures, business cards, stationery, misc.: $2,700.

Total Marketing Expense This Plan: $10,000.

Projected annual total sales are $91,000.

Marketing is approximately 11 percent of sales.

Income and Sales Targets

Our prices are based on a minimum daily consulting fee of $500 plus expenses. Our target sales figures are based on 3.5 days of time sold per week for one person. When we reach this average figure we will raise our rates to $600 per day. All consulting work has a one-day minimum fee. Any software or hardware sales we originate will include a 20 percent markup for our time and overhead.

Future Growth

We are in a growth business but recognize that it changes at a bewildering rate of speed, potentially

(continues)

rendering our knowledge obsolete. We will dedicate a significant portion of our time to continual
upgrading of our knowledge and services. We will
also dedicate time to developing products such as
training programs or seminars as profit centers to
expand our influence in the marketplace and
generate additional profits.

RESOURCES

BOOKS

General Business

Bermont, Hubert. *How to Become a Successful Consultant in Your Own Field*. Rocklin, Calif.: Prima, 1995. One of the best books on being self-employed I've come across. Excellent writing and a down-to-earth pragmatic viewpoint that makes sense no matter what business you're in. In a sense, all self-employed people work as consultants.

Hawken, Paul. *Growing a Business*. New York: Simon & Schuster. One of the best books out there for anyone starting a business. Entertaining and realistic. Highly Recommended.

Holtz, Herman. *How to Succeed as an Independent Consultant.* New York: Wiley, 1988. Good advice on consulting as a profession. Particularly good on working with the local, state, and federal governments.

General Marketing

Levinson, Jay Conrad. *Guerrilla Marketing: Secrets For Making Big Profits From Your Small Business.* Boston: Houghton Mifflin, 1993

—— *Guerrilla Marketing Attack.* Boston: Houghton Mifflin, 1989.

The Guerrilla series includes excellent general small-business marketing books. They are based on the premise that a creative small business marketer can beat out competition big and small by being innovative. Levinson gives many specific examples of tactics and strategy.

Bangs, David H., Jr. *Business Planning Guide.* Upstart Publishing Company, Inc., 1992.

—— *Market Planning Guide.* Upstart Publishing Company, Inc., 1992.

Excellent nuts-and-bolts, small business-oriented guides to writing and using business plans and marketing plans. Writing a business plan forces you to consider every aspect of going into business and becomes a necessary document if you ever need bank financing.

Accounting

Kamaroff, Bernard. *Small-Time Operator,* 20th ed. Bell Springs, 1995. Understanding cash flow, billing, profits, and the way money flows through your business is vital to making marketing decisions. *Small-Time Operator* is a classic how-to book for small business accounting. Accounting is a way of knowing how well you are doing at any given moment. Kamaroff shows you how to use it effectively without boring your pants off. Use his knowledge to learn to talk to your accountant (and save money!).

Direct Response and Direct Mail

Geller, Lois K. *The Complete Guide to Profitable Direct Marketing.* New York: The Free Press, 1996. A guide to small-business direct marketing that covers everything from copywriting techniques to online sales.

Bustiner, Irving. *Mail Order Selling: How To Market Almost Anything By Mail,* 3rd ed. New York: Wiley, 1995. A classic on using mail-order that includes many useful techniques, particularly on the use of classified advertising, even if you're not a mail-order business.

Sales

Gallagher, Bill, Orvel Ray Wilson, and Jay Conrad Levinson. *Guerrilla Selling.* Boston, Houghton Mifflin, 1992. Another Guerrilla book with a good—though often idealized—approach to sales.

Edic, Martin. *Sales for the Self-Employed.* Rocklin, Calif., Prima, 1997. The companion volume to this book—focusing on sales.

Advertising

Bruneau, Edmund A. *Rx (Prescription) for Advertising.* Boston: Boston Books, 1986. The book for the business owner considering the use of advertising to promote business. How to deal with writers, artists, agencies, media, and so on—written in a down-to-earth, expert voice.

The Franchise Business Model

Gerber, Michael. *The E Myth.* Harper Business, 1986. Interesting work on the concept of running your business as a system.

Inventions, Patents, Trademarks, Licensing

Tripp, Alan R. *Millions From The Mind*. New York: AMACOM, 1992. In spite of the silly title, this is the best book I've found on developing, protecting, and marketing your ideas and inventions.

MAGAZINES AND PERIODICALS

Inc. Magazine. A source of useful tips and advice from your peers. As with any of these resources, even one small but profitable idea easily justifies the price of a subscription or book.

In Business. Oriented toward companies with less than twenty-five employees including many one-person businesses.

MISCELLANEOUS

The Small Business Administration. Check your phone book under Federal Government to find the nearest office. They have many useful, free publications, can offer excellent help with planning and financing, and may hook you up with a Service Corps Of Retired Executives (SCORE) mentor who can help you find your way through the ins and outs of business management.

Modern Postcard, 6354 Corte del Abeto #E, Carlsbad, California 92009. Great prices and quality for color postcards and flyers.

ABC Pictures, Inc., 1867 East Florida Street, Springfield, Missouri 65803-4583. A good source for 8 × 10 black-and-white glossies of your work—in large quantities, cheap.

INDEX